What Do They Believe?

A Systematic Theology of the Major Western Religions

STRIVING for ETERNITY MINISTRIES

A Ministry of
Striving for Eternity Ministries
www.StrivingForEternity.org

Pastor Andrew R. Rappaport

Pastor Andrew R. Rappaport

ISBN: 978-0-9900011-1-9

Contents

Introduction

Introduction to World Religions

Why Study World Religions and Cults?

- To know what is believed in order to defend against false doctrines
- To recognize the deception that many people are under and seek to set them free with the gospel
- To protect against becoming deceived ourselves
- To protect our families and friends from false religions and cults
- To know the truth

Definition of a Cult

What is it that defines a cult versus a religion? Religion come from a Latin word which means to bind together. It is a reference for those human ways of integrating existence, of expressing meaning in an integrated universe. Religion is a set of systematic teachings or doctrines that reflect the ultimate order, meaning and possible transformation of existence for a people.

Although no one is certain of the word's origins, we know that 'religion' derives from Latin and that languages influenced by Latin have equivalents to the English word 'religion'. What in British scholarship was once called 'Comparative Religion' is known in Germany as Religionswissenschaft, religion's systematic study (or Wissenschaft), and in France it is known as les sciences religieuses. Although the ancient words to which we trace 'religion' had nothing to do with today's meanings—for it seems to have come from words that meant: to pay careful attention to some activity (religere) or to tie something tightly (religare)—it is today commonly used to refer to those beliefs, behaviours, and social institutions that have something to do with speculations on any, and all, of the following: the origin, end and significance of the universe; what happens after death; the existence and wishes of powerful, non-human beings such as spirits, ancestors, angels, demons and gods; and the manner in which all of this shapes human behaviour. Because each of these makes reference to an invisible (i.e. non-empirical) world that somehow lies outside of, or beyond, human history, the things we name as 'religious' are commonly thought to be opposed to those institutions that we label as 'political'. We therefore operate under the assumption that, whereas religion is a matter of personal belief that can never be settled by rational debate, such things as politics are observable, public and thus open to rational debate.[1]

Most religions have groups of cults that splinter off from the main religion. Commonly, a cult will have five traits which will differentiate it from its main religion. This study will look specifically at some of the cults that have splintered from Christianity.

1. Scripture twisting and de facto assertions of extra biblical revelation

> Use of Scripture is often with a disregard to context to justify unbiblical or extra biblical doctrines.

2. Authoritarianism

> Individual interpretation on subjects is not allowed. Only the cult leader(s) can interpret and they are accountable to no one.
>
> Most of the time a person or organization becomes the authority on the proper interpretation of the Scriptures. Some of these cults will state that only they can properly interpret the Scripture, and therefore, they can twist it and explain that the average person cannot understand without the cult. Therefore, if a person disagrees with the

interpretation based on a normal reading of the Scriptures the cult can have an answer that the individual cannot know on their own. Authoritarianism allows the cult authority to twist the Scriptures.

3. Exclusivism

Only the organization has the truth and all others are excluded from the truth.

4. Isolationism

Members of the organization are not to speak to outsiders about doctrine unless to convert them. The organization often states that it has the truth and wants to protect its members.

5. Endangerment

Another trait that many include is endangerment. It is true that most cults teaching's do lead to either physical or emotional endangerment of its members. This one trait may not be true for all cults.

What Is in This Study?

This is a careful study of some of the major world religions and cults. This study will quote original source material from those sources accepted as authoritative to each of the religions or material generally accepted by most in the religion. Many people study different religions, however they do not spend the time to understand these religions in their own context. Many study with the view to refute. This study will attempt to explain what the belief systems are within the context of the religion, not the Christian context. The areas of each study include:

1. View of Authority (Scriptures)

The view of authority will address those documents or people that the religion believes are authoritative. Some of these authorities are considered to be God's Word. It must also be studied as to how these religions acquired these authorities, which may include the view of inspiration and how they believe God's Word is revealed. The view of authority is the starting point for any religion because it gives the parameters of the belief system of the religion.

2. View of God (Trinity)

The view of God will address the nature and attributes of God in general where they disagree with Biblical Christianity. More specifically it will address the issues of the Godhead and view of the Trinity. The Trinity has become unique to Christianity in general; however, there are those that call themselves Christian that disbelieve in the Trinity.

3. View of Jesus Christ (Deity)

The view of Jesus Christ is the heartbeat of Christianity. The question is over His Deity. The view that Jesus Christ is God is unique to Christianity. However, since the early years of Christianity there was debate over His Deity and Humanity. Many, so called, "Christians" argue these same issues today.

4. View of Sin (Man's Spiritual Condition)

The view of sin is essential to understanding the religion's view of salvation. The core issue is man's spiritual condition. Is man born spiritually dead or neutral with the possibility to sin or do good and affected by his/her environment? How one views sin answers the question of how one views salvation and the purpose of it.

5. View of Salvation (How Does One Go to Heaven)

The view of salvation is the essential doctrine that differentiates Biblical Christianity from all other religions. Therefore, it is the most important topic in the study of world religions and cults. The question addressed is if man can work for salvation or not.

6. View of Eternal State (Heaven and Hell)

The view of eternal state is often the goal of salvation. The view of heaven, hell and any other final judgment differs between religions.

Chapter 1

Judaism

Authority

Judaism has four major sources of authority accepted today: Tanakh, Mishnah, Midrash and the Talmud.

Tanakh

The Tanakh is the Hebrew Bible containing 24 books. It is the Christian Old Testament with some books combined into one (i.e. 1 and 2 Samuel are one book called Samuel). It is referred to as the Written law and the belief is that God dictated the Bible to the writers word for word. There is a three-fold division to the Tanakh: Torah, Prophets and Writings.

Torah

Torah means law. In general, the Torah can refer to both the Oral and Written Law or the whole of the Tanakh. However, the Torah more specifically refers to the Pentateuch, which are the first five books of the Bible also called the books of Moses. The Torah is the most important of Jewish authorities.

Judaism teaches that every letter in the torah is identical to that which was given to Moses on Mount Sinai and it is complete.

> It follows from the perfection of the Torah that it can never be improved upon, and therefore God will never supersede it by another Revelation. This dogma of Judaism is deduced from the text, 'It is not in heaven' (Deut. 30:12), which is expounded thus: 'That you shall not say another Moses will arise and bring us another Torah from heaven, I have already made it known to you that "it is not in

> heaven," i.e. there is nothing left of it in heaven' (Deut. R. 8:6).[2]

The creation of the Torah is believed to have preceded Creation.

> Seven things were created before the world was created: Torah, repentance, the Garden of Eden (i.e. Paradise), Gehinnom, the Throne of Glory, the Temple, and the name of the Messiah. (Pes. 54a)

Jews would see the Christians as having multiple New Testament Bibles, referring to the different manuscripts. They believe that proves that the New Testament cannot be from God because of the differences in the manuscripts.

The passage above referring to "supersede it by another Revelation" is thought to be a veiled reference to the New Testament. Below is another example.

> Although, the Torah was created before Creation there is debate over how long before. According to one opinion, 'the Torah preceded Creation by two thousand years' (Gen. R. 8:2); but another view is, 'Nine hundred and seventy-four generations before creation of the world the Torah was written and lay in the bosom of the Holy One, blessed be He' (ARN 31).

Prophets

The Prophets contain the major and minor prophets.

Hayiographa or the Writings

The Writings are the rest of the writings of the Old Testament Bible (i.e. Psalm, Proverbs, Samuel, etc.).

Midrash

The Midrash is a commentary on the Tanakh. Some Rabbis state that it is the system of interpretation employed throughout the Rabbinic literature.[3] Hence, the allegorical method of interpretation in the Midrash leads to some Jewish mysticism. There are several different Midrash's written by different Rabbis. They are not assumed to be the Word of God, but they are an authoritive source of Judaism.

Mishnah

The Mishnah is an abstract or summary of the religious and civil law of the Jews. It is referred to as the (Oral Law). It is believed that the oral law was given at the same time as the written law on Mount Sinai and was given to Moses but not written down until about 220 B.C.E.

Judaism teaches that the Mishnah was memorized concept by concept as opposed to word-by-word throughout the centuries. The concepts given to Moses are preserved in what are now over 1100 pages.

The Mishnah was given orally from generation to generation but not word for word, instead concept by concept.

Jacob Neusner states in his translation of the Mishnah:

> The Mishnah itself is generally supposed to have come to closure at the end of the second century, and its date, for conventional purposes only, is ca. A.D. 200. Now, of these two groups—sages from 70–130, and from 135–200—the latter is represented far more abundantly than the former. . . .
>
> In the aftermath of the war against Rome in A.D.132–135, the Temple was declared permanently prohibited to Jews, and Jerusalem was closed off to them as well. So there was no cult, no Temple, no holy city, to which, at this time, the description of the Mishnaic laws applied. They observe at the very outset, therefore, that a sizable proportion of the Mishnah deals with matters to which the sages had no material access or practical knowledge at the time of their work.
>
> A fundamental issue with the Rabbis was the acceptance of a traditional Torah, transmitted from one generation to another by word of mouth, side by side with the written text. It was claimed that the Oral Torah equally with the

Written Torah, goes back to the Revelation on Sinai, if not in detail at least in principle. Forty-two enactments, which find no record in the Pentateuch, are described by the Talmud as 'laws given to Moses on Sinai'.

The Roman governor Quietus asked R. Gamaliel, 'How many Toroth were given to Israel?' He answered, 'Two—one in writing and the other orally'" (Sifre Deut. 351:145a).

Why, however, was it necessary for the Torah to be given in this twofold form? An answer suggested to the question is: "The Holy One, blessed be He, gave Israel two Toroth, the written and the oral. He gave them the Written Torah in which are six hundred and thirteen commandments in order to fill them with precepts whereby they could earn merit. He gave them the Oral Torah whereby they could be distinguished from the other nations. This was not given in writing, so that the Ishmaelites should not fabricate it as they have done the Written Torah and say that they were Israel" (Num. R. 14:10). In the word 'Ishmaelites' we must detect one of the substitutions which were employed in the Middle-Ages to circumvent the censor. Obviously, Christians are meant. Since the Church adopted the Hebrew Scriptures, they ceased to be the peculiar possession of Jews. Therefore, the Oral Torah, which was not accepted by the Church, safeguarded the distinctiveness of the Jewish people living in a Christian environment. The problem with the word 'Ishmaelites' referring to Christians is that by the seventh century the Muslims (Arabs descendants of Ishmael) ruled the area of Israel and Islam tried to unite the two but Judaism would not conform causing Muhammad to split from the use of the Hebrew Scriptures. So depending on when it was written it could have been referring to either or both the Christians and Muslims.

Talmud

The Talmud is a commentary on the Mishnah. The Talmud is a work wherein is deposited the bulk of the literary labours of numerous Jewish scholars over a period of some 700 years, roughly speaking, between 200 B.C.E. and 500 C.E. There are two primary Talmud's; the Palestinian and the Babylonian.

1. *Palestinian Talmud*—composed shortly after 400 C.E.

2. *Babylonian Talmud*—referred as the Talmud, completed about 500 C.E.

> The Talmud, for the Jew, is not merely a great literary production, which it is. It is not merely a great repository of law and ritual, which it is. The Talmud is a great fund of Jewish religious experience and wisdom accumulated throughout the course of the ages. *The Talmud ranks next to the Sacred Scriptures* in significance as a source for religious insight, inspiration and practice, and will instruct the last generations of mankind.[4] (emphasis added)

The religious leaders of each generation were empowered through the Mishnah to legislate for their own time in the light of contemporary circumstances. Therefore, the Torah, both written and oral, were static and unchanging. However, the Talmud and Midrash were a running commentary on the Torah, both written and oral.

The Talmud is their tradition and usually seems to take precedence over the Scriptures for faith and practice. This is thought to be so that if the law is forgotten the tradition will not be and sometime later someone will ask the reason for the tradition and the law will then be remembered.

Rabbinic Law

Rabbinic law are the rules of the rabbis found in the Talmud and the Midrash. It is important to note that ritual keeping is essential to Judaism. Jewish rabbis believe that the ritual keeps the message over time. The message of the Torah could be lost over time, but if tied to the ritual eventually someone somewhere will question the meaning of the ritual and regain the message from the ritual.

The Sadducees did not accept the Rabbinical law found in the Midrash, Mishnah or Talmud. There was a spilt in the Jewish leadership when the Jews returned from exile. The Rabbis claimed that the oral law was given to Moses on Mount Sinai and is God's Word. The Sadducees taught that there was not such law given, but that it was traditions held by the Rabbis.

There was political battle between the Sadducees and Pharisees (Rabbis). The Sadducees had the High Priest as the head of their group giving them authority. Therefore, the Pharisees/Rabbis had the Rabbinical Law which gave them authority. Hence, the need for writing down of the oral law for the people was necessary, to give the Pharisees an authority.

God

The conception of God held by the Rabbis is monotheistic in the strictest degree.

> He created in the beginning one man only, so that heretics should not say that there are several Powers in heaven (Sanh. 38a).
>
> On the verse *"Hear, O Israel, the Lord our God, the Lord is one"* the comment is made: "The Holy One, blessed be He, said to Israel, 'My children, everything that I created in the Universe in is pairs—e.g. heaven and earth, the sun and moon, Adam and Eve, this world and the World to Come; but I am one and alone in the Universe' (Deut. R. II. 31).

The Rabbi's define the Christian Trinity as three gods in one God, as can be seen in their attempt to answer the Christian doctrine of God.

> What of that which is written, 'Let us make man in *our* image, after *our* likeness' (Gen 1:26)? ... Read what follows: it is not said, 'And gods created man in their image,' but 'And God created man in His own image. ... In the past Adam was created from the dust of the ground and Eve was created from Adam. Henceforward it is to be 'in our image, after our likeness'—meaning, man will not be able to come into existence without woman, not woman

> without man, not both without the *Sheckinah.'* (R. Simlai asked by the Minim) (emphasis original).[5]

The Sheckinah explains 'our' to mean God in addition to man and women; i.e. each human being is formed from three parents; a threefold parentage (Nid. 31a). The threefold parentage being man, woman and God. This is the Jewish explanation to the plural noun usage.

Jesus Christ

Jesus as Moshiach (Messiah)

Judaism states that the virgin birth is a myth and that Jesus Christ is a false prophet according to Deuteronomy 13:6.

> *If your brother, the son of your mother, your son or your daughter, the wife of your bosom, or your friend who is as your own soul, secretly entices you, saying, 'Let us go and serve other gods,' which you have not known, neither you nor your fathers,* (Deuteronomy 13:6)

Judaism teaches that the phrase *"the son of your mother"* is a veiled reference to Jesus Christ as an apostate that would lead Israel to other gods and claim to be born of a virgin (without a human father). The context of the passage is addressing false prophets.

Jewish Concept of Moshiach

If Jesus is not the Jewish Moshiach, then what is the Jewish concept of Moshiach?

The general belief was that the sending of the Moshiach was part of the Creator's plan at the inception of the Universe. 'Seven things were created before the world was created: Torah, repentance, the Garden of Eden (i.e. Paradise), Gehinnom, the Throne of Glory, the Temple, and the name of the Messiah' (Pes. 54a). In a later work, there is the observation: 'From the beginning of the creation of the world king Messiah was born, for he entered the mind (of God) before even the world was created' (Pesikta Rab. 152b).

On one point the Rabbis were unanimous, viz. Moshiach would be just a human being divinely appointed to carry out an allotted task. The Talmud nowhere indicated a belief in a superhuman Deliverer as the Moshiach. The prevailing belief was that the Moshiach would be a descendant of the king, and a common designation for him in Rabbinic literature is 'the son of David'.

Remember, however, that the Talmud was written after the time of Christ and has the purpose to answer current circumstances. The Talmud had to address the division between Judaism and Christianity and the distinction was in a Divine Moshiach.

> As against the belief that God had determined an exact date for the dawn of the Messianic era, there grew up another doctrine that the date was not fixed but would be affected by the conduct of the people. That thought was read into the words, 'I the Lord will hasten it in its time' (Is. 60:22), which were explained in this sense: 'If you are worthy I will hasten it; if you are not worthy it will be in its time' (Sanh. 98a).

This answers the question why did the Messiah not come after 483 years of the rebuilding of the city and temple as Daniel prophesied (Daniel 9:24-27). God is now waiting until His people (the Jews) are ready, as defined by doing Torah.

An elaborate description of the effect which the Messianic era will have upon the state of the world is contained in this extract: 'Ten things will the Holy One, blessed be he, renew in the Hereafter: 1) he will illumine the world; as it is said, "The sun shall be no more thy light by day, neither for brightness shall the moon give light unto thee; but the Lord shall be unto thee an everlasting light" (Is. 60:19). 2) He will cause running water to issue from Jerusalem, and whoever has an ailment will find healing there. 3) He will cause trees to produce their fruit every month and all persons will eat of them and be healed. 4) All ruined cities will be rebuilt and no waste place will remain in the world. 5) He will rebuild Jerusalem with sapphires. 6) Peace will reign throughout nature. 7) He will assemble all beasts, birds, and reptiles, and make a covenant between them and all Israel. 8) Weeping and wailing will cease in the world. 9) Death will cease in the world. 10) There will be no more sighing, groaning, or anguish, but all will be happy.

Sin

Pre-existence of Man

Judaism teaches that God created all the souls of man on the same day with the angels. 'In the seventh heaven, *Araboth*, are stored the spirits and souls which have still to be created' (Chag. 12b), i.e. the unborn souls which have yet to be united to bodies.

The soul is the spiritual force within man which raises him above an animal existence, inspires him with ideas and prompts him to choose the good and reject the evil. Since the spirit of man was created prior to the fall it is good and not sinful.

Evil Impulse

They make God the author of sin. "The Holy One, blessed be He, said to Israel, My children, I have created the evil impulse, and I have created the Torah as an antidote to it; if you occupy yourselves with Torah you will not be delivered into its power" (Kid. 30b).

When God created man, he was created good but with an evil impulse. "The Holy One, blessed be He, created two impulses, one good and the other evil" (Ber.61a).

At the root of the discussion was the opinion that man is essentially a sinful creature who is bound during his lifetime to do many deeds which earn for him the condemnation of God. Part of human nature is the evil impulse, which can be mastered, but all too often takes control and demoralizes.

The belief that in every human being there are two urges—one to evil and the other to goodness—figures prominently in Rabbinic ethics. Having to find a basis for the doctrine in the text of the Bible, the Rabbis deduced it in this way: 'What means that which is written, "Then the Lord God formed man" (Gen. 2:7), the wajjitzer (and He formed) being spelt with two letters j? The Holy One, blessed be He, created two impulses, one good and the other evil' (Ber.61a). The Hebrew word for 'impulse' is Jetzer; hence the two j's were then to indicate two—the Jetzer Tob, 'good impulse' and Jetzer Hara, 'evil impulse'.

The evil impulse is thirteen years older than the good impulse. It exists from the time of a person's emergence from his mother's womb; it grows with him and accompanies him through life. It begins to desecrate the Sabbath, to kill and act immorally, but there is nothing (within him) to prevent it. After thirteen years the good impulse is born. When he desecrates the Sabbath it warns him, "Good-for-nothing! Behold it is said, 'Every one that profaneth it shall surely be put to death' (Exodus 31:14). What is significant about the age of thirteen? It is the year that a boy would be recognized as a man after his Bar-Mitzvah.

The Talmud in an attempt to prevent the teaching of perfectionism allows sin as long as it is done in private (emphasising the outward appearance not the inward heart).

> If a man sees that his evil impulse is gaining the mastery over him, let him go to a place where he is unknown, put on black clothes and do what his heart desires; but let him not profane the Name publicly." (Chag. 16a)

In other words sin, as long as it is in private and other people do not know about it is permissible. It does not answer the heart issue nor that God knows about it. A private sin still profanes the name of God.

Many utterances can be adduced from the Talmud to prove that man is sinless by nature. 'A child aged one year who, has not tasted sin' (Joma 22b). Upon the words of Ecclesiastes, 'There is a time to be born and a time to die' (Eccles. 3:2), was based on` the aspiration, 'Happy the man whose hour of death is like the hour of his birth; as at his birth he is free of sin, so at his death may he be free of sin' (p. Ber. 4d).

Free Will

Judaism has the belief that all men have a sinful impulse not a sinful nature and therefore they have a “free” will. People are born morally neutral not desiring good or evil. God does not decide if a man is righteous or wicked it is wholly the will of man. “The angel appointed over conception is named Laiah. He takes a seminal drop, sets it before the Holy One, blessed be He, and asks, ‘Sovereign of the Universe! what is to become of this drop? Is it to develop into a person strong or weak, wise or foolish, rich or poor?’ But no mention is made of its becoming wicked or righteous” (Nid. 16b). An oft-quoted maxim reads: “All is in the hands of Heaven except the fear of Heaven” (Ber. 33b), which means that although God decides the fate of the individual, a reservation is made with respect to the moral character of his life. It is the moral character that they base righteous and wickedness on and not the relationship with God, because all Jews believe that they are born into a relationship with God.

The conviction that man’s will is unfettered is seen to be the foundation of Rabbinic ethics. The nature of his life is molded by his desires. He *can* misuse life’s opportunities if he so wishes, but in no circumstance would it be agreed that he *must* misuse them. The evil impulse constantly tempts him; but if he falls, the responsibility is his and his alone.

A curious explanation is given why the whole human race originated from one man: ‘Because of the righteous and the wicked, that the righteous should not say, “We are the descendants of a righteous ancestor,” and the wicked say, “We are the descendants of a wicked ancestor”’(Sanh. 38a). The moral is that neither can plead hereditary influence as the deciding factor in their character.

Salvation

Salvation from Sin?

Salvation is through the Torah. This is the importance of the Torah for a Jew. A Jew has two issues to overcome: heritage (being born a Jew) and the belief that there is no sin nature in man and therefore, man can choose good on his/her own. Jews do not see themselves as sinners by nature. Their tradition and heritage convinces them that they do not have a need for a saviour. They believe they can master the evil impulse and they can do that which pleases God through repentance.

Salvation by Repentance

Inasmuch as God created man with the evil impulse, by reason of which he is prone to sin, justice demanded that an antidote should likewise be provided for salvation. If wickedness is a disease to which the human being is susceptible, it was necessary for him to have a medium of healing. Such is to be found in repentance.

Why, however, was it necessary for the Torah to be given in this twofold form? An answer suggested to the question is:

> The Holy One, blessed be He, gave Israel two Toroth, the written and the oral. He gave them the Written Torah in which are six hundred and thirteen commandments in order to fill them with precepts whereby *they could earn merit*. He gave them the Oral Torah whereby they could be distinguished from the other nations. This was not given in writing, so that the Ishmaelites should not fabricate it as they have done the Written Torah and say that they were Israel' (Num. R. 14:10). (emphasis added)

Clearly, the Jew believes that living according to the Torah's 613 laws will earn them merit.

Since, as the Bible declares, God delights not in the death of the wicked but that he turn from his evil way and live (Ezekiel 33:11), it follows that He is anxious for man to repent and facilitates his endeavour to do so.

The Rabbis declared that repentance was one of the seven things which were created by God before the world itself was formed. 'Seven things were before the Universe came into being. They are: Torah, repentance, Paradise, Gehinnom, the Throne of Glory, the Sanctuary, and the name of the Messiah' (Pes. 54a).

> Great is repentance for it reaches to the Throne of Glory. Great is repentance, for it makes the Redemption (by the Messiah) to come near. Great is repentance, for it lengthens the years of a man's life (Joma 86a et seq).
>
> There is nothing greater than repentance (Deut. R. 2:24).
>
> Better is one hour of repentance and good deeds in this world than the whole life of the World to Come (Aboth 4:22).
>
> Neither sin-offering nor trespass-offering nor death nor the Day of Atonement can bring expiation without repentance (Tosifta Joma v. 9).
>
> Whence is it derived that if one repents, it is imputed to him as if he had gone up to Jerusalem, built the Temple, erected an altar and offered upon it all the sacrifices enumerated in the Torah? From the text, 'The sacrifices of God are a broken spirit' (Ps. 51:17) (Lev. R. 7:2).
>
> Man best qualifies himself in the vestibule for the pure, spiritual atmosphere of 'the hall' by devoting himself to the study and practice of the precepts revealed by God. 'He who has acquired for himself words of Torah has acquired for himself life in the World to Come' (Aboth 2:8).

What was the message that John the Baptist preached? Repentance!

Gentile Salvation

Salvation for the Gentile is through obedience to the Noahic covenant.

Eternal State

The World to Come

Many incidental remarks occur in the Talmud declaring that the person who performs a certain action will, or will not, have a share in the World to Come.

As for those who are to be included, we are told:

> Who will inherit the World to Come? He who joins the benediction "Blessed art Thou Who hast redeemed Israel" to the Eighteen Benedictions (Ber. 4b).
>
> Whoever recites Ps 145 thrice daily may be assured that he is a son of the World to Come. The reason is that it contains the verse, "Thou openest Thy hand and satisfiest every living thing with favour" (verse 16) (Ber. 4b).
>
> Whoever says the benediction (in the Grace after meals) over a full cup of wine will be granted a boundless inheritance and will be worthy to inherit two worlds, this world and the World to Come (Ber. 51a).
>
> Among those who will inherit the World to Come are: who resides in the land of Israel and who rears his son in the study of the Torah (Pes.113a).
>
> Whoever walks a distance of four cubits in the land of Israel is assured of being a son of the World to Come (Keth. 111a).
>
> He who studies the laws of Judaism is assured of being a son of the World to Come (Meg. 28b).
>
> They sent a question from Palestine to the Rabbis in Babylon, "Who will be a son of the World to Come?" They answered, "He who is meek and humble, walks about with a lowly demeanour, studies the Torah constantly, and takes no credit to himself" (Sanh. 88b).

As for those who are to be excluded, we are told:

> Whoever crosses a stream behind a woman will have no share in the World to Come (Ber. 61a).
>
> Who puts his fellow-man to shame in public will have no share in the World to Come (B.M. 59a).
>
> Seven classes of persons will have no share in the World to Come: a scribe, a teacher of children, the best of physicians, the judge of a city, an enchanter, a synagogue beadle, and a butcher (ARN 36).[6]
>
> In the Hereafter, the Holy One, blessed be He, will take a Scroll of the Torah, set it upon His lap and say, "Let him who occupied himself therewith come and receive his reward. (A.Z. 2a).
>
> In the Hereafter the Holy One, blessed be He, will judge the righteous and wicked of Israel. To the righteous, He will grant a permit for them to enter Gan Eden and the wicked he will send back to Gehinnom. ... After that He will restore the righteous to Gan Eden and the wicked to Gehinnom' (Midrash to Ps 31:120a).
>
> In preparation for the Day of Judgement a record is kept of all that the human being does while on earth. 'All your deeds are written in a book' (Aboth 2:1).
>
> The following have no share in the World to Come: He who says that the doctrine of the Resurrection is not deducible from the Torah, who maintains that the Torah does not come from Heaven, and the epicurean. R. Akiba says, also he who reads non-canonical books, and who utters a spell over a wound, citing, "I will put none of the diseases upon thee which I have put upon the Egyptians, for I am the Lord that healeth thee" (Exodus 15:26). Abba Saul says, Also he who pronounces the Totragrammaton as it is written' (Sanh. 10:1).

There is not a dogmatic verdict on the eternal fate of a person. The many remarks are nothing more than a hyperbolical expression of approval or disapproval. More importance is, however, attached to the extract: 'All Israel has a share in the World to Come, as it is for ever' (Is. 60:21).

Gehinnom

The fate of the wicked is to descend into a place of punishment called Gehinnom or hell. Its origin predates the creation of the Universe (Pes. 54a). The principal safeguard, however, is the study of Torah. 'The fire of Gehinnom has no power over the disciples of the Sages. ... fire of Gehinnom has no power over the sinners in Israel.' (Chag. 27a) There is some debate between the Rabbi's on the subject of people being sent to Gehinnom for eternity or just for a time or not at all.

The principal element which exists there for the torment of the sinful is fire, but a fire of abnormal intensity. '[Ordinary] fire is a sixtieth of [the fire of] Gehinnom' (Ber. 57b). Another element which abounds there is brimstone. Finally, it is full of smoke.

R. Simeon b. Lakish, who lived in the third century, declared: 'There is no Gehinnom in the Hereafter; but the Holy One, blessed be he, will remove the sun from its sheath and blacken (the world with its fierce rays). The wicked will be punished and the righteous healed thereby' (A.Z. 3b).

Does the Talmud teach eternal punishment? There is at least one passage where such a doctrine seems to be implied. (Ber. 28b). ... [There is a] reluctance on the part of the Rabbis to think of an endless punishment. One authority declared: 'All who descend to Gehinnom will ascend except three: he who has intercourse with another man's wife, he who puts his fellow to shame in public, and he who calls his fellow by an opprobrious nickname' (B.M. 58b). ... 'The School of Shammai declared, There are three classes with respect to the Day of Judgement: the perfectly righteous, the completely wicked, and the average people. Those in the first class are forthwith inscribed and sealed for eternal life. Those in the second class are forthwith inscribed and sealed for Gehinnom. ... The third class will descend to Gehinnom and cry out (from the pains endured there) and then ascend; as it is said, "I will bring the third part through fire, and will refine them as silver is refined, and will try them as gold is tried; they shall call on My name and I will hear them" (Zech. 13:9). ... The sinners of Israel with their bodies and the sinners of the Gentiles with their bodies descend to Gehinnom and are judged there for twelve months. After twelve months their bodies are destroyed, and their souls burnt and scattered by a wind under the soles of the feet of the righteous.' (R.H. 16b et seq.).

Chapter 2

Roman Catholicism

This chapter will reference the 1995 "Catechism of the Catholic Church" for its quotations. This document is the latest printing from the Roman Catholic Church (RCC) and is used to summarize its beliefs. All numbers referenced will refer to paragraph numbers in the "Catechism of the Catholic Church".

Authority

The Roman Catholic Church understands three sources of authority:

1. Tradition

2. Scripture

3. The Church

It is clear therefore that, in the supremely wise arrangement of God, sacred Tradition, Sacred Scripture and the Magisterium of the Church are so connected and associated that one of them cannot stand without the others. Working together, each in its own way, under the action of the one Holy Spirit, they all contribute effectively to the salvation of souls (95).

Notice the order of the RCC authority. Tradition often precedes Scripture as an authority (95, 97). This may be caused by the RCC view that tradition interprets Scripture, not Scripture interpreting tradition (113, 128).

Tradition

The RCC believes that God provided two forms of transmitting the Gospel: oral and written (76). The oral is a living transmission called tradition (78, 126). The RCC clearly believes that all revealed truths are not from the Scriptures alone but include tradition (81-82, 84, 95). “Sacred Tradition and Sacred Scripture make up a single sacred deposit of the Word of God.” (97)

See the paragraphs below that were referenced above:

> The Gospel was handed on ... orally “by the apostles who handed on, by the spoken word of their preaching, by the example they gave, by the institutions they established, what they themselves had received—whether from the lips of Christ, from his way of life and his works, or whether they had learned it at the prompting of the Holy Spirit” (76)
>
> This living transmission, accomplished in the Holy Spirit, is called Tradition, ... Through Tradition, "the Church, in her doctrine, life and worship, perpetuates and transmits to every generation all that she herself is, all that she believes. (78)
>
> "And [Holy] Tradition transmits in its entirety the Word of God which has been entrusted to the apostles by Christ the Lord and the Holy Spirit. (81)
>
> As a result the Church, to whom the transmission and interpretation of Revelation is entrusted, "does not derive her certainty about all revealed truths from the holy Scriptures alone. Both Scripture and Tradition must be accepted and honoured with equal sentiments of devotion and reverence.(82)
>
> The apostles entrusted the "Sacred deposit" of the faith (the depositum fidei), contained in Sacred Scripture and Tradition, to the whole of the Church. ... So, in maintaining, practising and professing the faith that has been handed on, there should be a remarkable harmony between the bishops and the faithful.(84)

> Read the Scripture within "the living Tradition of the whole Church". According to a saying of the Fathers, Sacred Scripture is written principally in the Church's heart rather than in documents and records, for the Church carries in her Tradition the living memorial of God's Word, and it is the Holy Spirit who gives her the spiritual interpretation of the Scripture (113)

> The oral tradition. "For, after the ascension of the Lord, the apostles handed on to their hearers what he had said and done, but with that fuller understanding which they, instructed by the glorious events of Christ and enlightened by the Spirit of truth, now enjoyed." (126)

The RCC view of tradition affects the manner in which they interpret the Scriptures.

> [T]he Church carries in her Tradition the living memorial of God's Word, and it is the Holy Spirit who gives her the spiritual interpretation of the Scripture. (113)

> [C]onstantly in her Tradition, has illuminated the unity of the divine plan in the two Testaments through typology. (128)

There is a note that distinguishes between Church Tradition and local church tradition.

> Tradition is to be distinguished from the various theological, disciplinary, liturgical or devotional traditions, born in the local churches over time. These are the particular forms, adapted to different places and times, in which the great Tradition is expressed. In the light of Tradition, these traditions can be retained, modified or even abandoned under the guidance of the Church's Magisterium. (83)

Scriptures

Along with RCC tradition the RCC accept the Scriptures as an equal authority (82, 84, 95, 97). The RCC believes that it had a role in the accepting and giving of the canon of Scripture (138,

2030). In other words, we would not have a set collection or list of which books are inspired or not inspired without the RCC. This view is to say that the authority of the church was required to decide which books were in and which were out of the Bible. Furthermore, the RCC has accepted additional books, chapters and passages not in the Protestant Bible.

> It was by the apostolic Tradition that the Church discerned which writings are to be included in the list of the sacred books. This complete list is called the canon of Scripture. It includes 46 books for the Old Testament (45 if we count Jeremiah and Lamentations as one) and 27 for the New. (120)

The RCC believes that the Church is the only authority that can determine which books make up the Bible, therefore, the Protestants lack the whole of Scripture.

> The Church accepts and venerates as inspired the 46 books of the Old Testament and the 27 books of the New. (138)

Further is the view of interpreting Christ in the Old Testament.

> All Sacred Scripture is but one book, and that one book is Christ, because all divine Scripture speaks of Christ, and all divine Scripture is fulfilled in Christ (134)

It should be noted historically that the Jews had a list of the books of the Canon for hundreds of years before the RCC developed their list. The earliest known complete Old Testament list was discussed at the council of Jamnia in about 90 A.D. The council of Jamnia was a meeting of Rabbi's where they answered the issues of which of the Old Testament books were part of the Old Testament. The issue of note was that the Old Testament books that the RCC accepts as the apocryphal books were not part of the Jewish canon. They were books of historical value that were placed in the back of the Old Testament. However, the RCC moved them into their chorological placement and called them Scripture.

The Church

The RCC sets itself up the only true “church” (838, 866). There is no Protestant church that is part of the “church”, because only the RCC fulfills the purpose and has the authority of the “church”.

Only the RCC can provide:

- the Scriptures (2030)
- grace through sacraments
- an example of holiness
- announce the saving truth (2032)
- announce moral principles
- make judgments on human affairs
- make present and manifest the visible sign of communion between God and men (1071)

The RCC is the only true “church” because of its authority. The RCC believes that it is holy and infallible (869, 891, 1426), therefore, it must have complete authority. The authority of the RCC is not rooted in their holiness or infallibility, but instead in their apostolic succession and function (the Magisterium).

See the paragraphs below that were referenced above:

> The Church is one: she acknowledges one Lord, confesses one faith, is born of one Baptism, forms only one Body, is given life by the one Spirit, for the sake of one hope (cf. Eph 4:3-5), at whose fulfillment all divisions will be overcome. (866)
>
> The Church is ultimately one, holy, catholic, and apostolic in her deepest and ultimate identity, because it is in her that "the Kingdom of heaven," the "Reign of God," already exists and will be fulfilled at the end of time. (865)

From the Church [the baptized] receives the Word of God ... From the Church he receives the grace of the sacraments that sustains him on the "way." From the Church he learns the example of holiness and recognizes its model and source in the all-holy Virgin Mary; he discerns it in the authentic witness of those who live it; he discovers it in the spiritual tradition and long history of the saints who have gone before him and whom the liturgy celebrates in the rhythms of the sanctoral cycle. (2030)

The Church ... has received this solemn command of Christ from the apostles to announce the saving truth. To the Church belongs the right always and everywhere to announce moral principles, including those pertaining to the social order, and to make judgments on any human affairs to the extent that they are required by the fundamental rights of the human person or the salvation of souls. (2032)

It makes the Church present and manifests her as the visible sign of the communion in Christ between God and men. (1071)

The liturgy is the summit toward which the activity of the Church is directed; it is also the font from which all [the church's] power flows. (1074)

As she has done for the canon of Sacred Scripture and for the doctrine of the faith, the Church, by the power of the Spirit who guides her into all truth, has gradually recognized this treasure received from Christ and, as the faithful steward of God's mysteries, has determined its dispensation. (1117)

The Church ... is upheld infallibly in the truth. (869)

The infallibility promised to the Church is also present in the body of bishops. ... When the Church through its supreme Magisterium proposes a doctrine for belief as being divinely revealed, and as the teaching of Christ, the definitions must be adhered to with the obedience of faith.

> This infallibility extends as far as the deposit of divine Revelation itself. (891)
>
> The Church herself, the Bride of Christ, is holy and without blemish. (1426)
>
> Reconciliation with the Church is inseparable from reconciliation with God. (1445)

The local bishops have authority of the local church but only as they receive it from the RCC (834, 894-895, 877).

> The bishops, as vicars and legates of Christ, govern the particular Churches assigned to them by their counsels, exhortations, and example, but over and above that also by the authority and sacred power. The power which they exercise personally in the name of Christ, is proper, ordinary, and immediate, although its exercise is ultimately controlled by the supreme authority of the Church. (894-895)
>
> Bishops will always strive to discern new gifts of consecrated life granted to the Church by the Holy Spirit; the approval of new forms of consecrated life is reserved to the Apostolic See. (919)

However, it is clearer in the fact that the RCC displays a tight relationship between itself and God (2039). In fact, to be at odds with the RCC is to be at odds with God (1445).

> To believe that the Church is "holy" and "catholic," and that she is "one" and "apostolic", is inseparable from belief in God, the Father, the Son, and the Holy Spirit. In the Apostles' Creed we profess "one Holy Church", and not to believe in the Church, so as not to confuse God with his works and to attribute clearly to God's goodness all the gifts he has bestowed on his Church. (750)

Apostolic Succession

Apostolic succession is the belief that there is a direct line from the apostles handed down to bishops in direct succession (77, 816, 860, 862-863, 869, 935-936, 1313, 1341, 1575). This succession is an office in the church held by few and is believed to have been established from the beginning of the church in an unbroken line (1555). This office gives certain men authority and power of the Apostles, which is to be different then the authority or power of other Christians (1023, 1087).

It is this belief that the RCC teaches that the Pope is a successor of Peter and therefore has ultimate authority on earth over the "church" (870, 880-884, 937, 1560, 1594). Furthermore, as Peter's successor, the Pope is infallible, like the RCC (891-892).

Apostolic succession is a key ingredient to understanding the RCC. This doctrine is where they attempt to get their authority and control of the people. It is this doctrine that will later link to the view that the RCC has the power and right to dispense salvation and forgiveness of sins. Yet there is no Scripture that teaches that there would continue to be an apostolic line, this doctrine was developed by RCC tradition.

The entire belief system of the RCC is based on this one doctrine. This is a case where the RCC view of tradition interpreting Scripture affects greatly the result of doctrine. It is their tradition that teaches the doctrine of apostolic succession and it must be true according to the RCC because their Magisterium teach it to be so. However, the Magisterium are part of this apostolic succession, so it is a circular argument.

These paragraphs are only some of the ones that describe the RCC view of their apostolic succession.

> In order that the full and living Gospel might always be preserved in the Church the apostles left bishops as their successors. They gave them their own position of teaching authority."[35] Indeed, "the apostolic preaching, which is expressed in a special way in the inspired books, was to be preserved in a continuous line of succession until the end of time. (77)

> [T]he Catholic Church, which is governed by the successor of Peter and by the bishops in communion with him. (816)

> [T]he apostles took care to appoint successors. (860)

Just as the office which the Lord confided to Peter alone, as first of the apostles, destined to be transmitted to his successors, is a permanent one, so also endures the office, which the apostles received, of shepherding the Church, a charge destined to be exercised without interruption by the sacred order of bishops. ... Hence the Church teaches that the bishops have by divine institution taken the place of the apostles as pastors of the Church,

The whole Church is apostolic, in that she remains, through the successors of St. Peter and the other apostles, in communion of faith and life with her origin: and in that she is "sent out" into the whole world. (862-863)

Divine assistance is also given to the successors of the apostles, teaching in communion with the successor of Peter, and, in a particular way, to the bishop of Rome, pastor of the whole Church, when, without arriving at an infallible definition and without pronouncing in a "definitive manner," they propose in the exercise of the ordinary Magisterium a teaching that leads to better understanding of Revelation in matters of faith and morals. (892)

Amongst those various offices which have been exercised in the Church from the earliest times the chief place, according to the witness of tradition, is held by the function of those who, through their appointment to the dignity and responsibility of bishop, and in virtue consequently of the unbroken succession going back to the beginning, are regarded as transmitters of the apostolic line. (1555)

The Church is apostolic because she is founded on the apostlos, in three ways:

she was and remains built on the foundation of the Apostles, the witnesses chosen and sent on mission by Christ himself;

with the help of the Spirit dwelling in her, the Church keeps and hands on the teaching, the "good deposit," the salutary words she has heard from the apostles;

> she continues to be taught, sanctified, and guided by the apostles until Christ's return, through their successors in pastoral office: the college of bishops, "assisted by priests, in union with the successor of Peter, the Church's supreme pastor. (857)

Magisterium

The Magisterium are the third great pillar of authority of the RCC (95). They get their authority from their apostolic succession. They guide (67, 93), teach (77, 85-86, 873, 2034, 2050), sanctify (873), govern (873) and exercise the authority (88) of the RCC. The Holy Spirit is known in the church's Magisterium, which He assists (688). They are without error (92). It is the Magisterium who have the sole responsibility and authority to interpret tradition and Scripture (85-86, 100, 119, 1008).

> The task of interpreting the Word of God authentically has been *entrusted solely to the Magisterium* of the Church, that is, to the Pope and to the bishops in communion with him. (100) (emphasis added)

See the paragraphs below that were referenced above:

> The task of giving an authentic interpretation of the Word of God, whether in its written form or in the form of Tradition, has been entrusted to the living teaching office of the Church alone. ... This means that the task of interpretation has been entrusted to the bishops in communion with the successor of Peter, the Bishop of Rome. Yet this Magisterium is not superior to the Word of God, but is its servant. It teaches only what has been handed on to it. At the divine command and with the help of the Holy Spirit, it listens to this devotedly, guards it with dedication and expounds it faithfully. All that it proposes for belief as being divinely revealed is drawn from this single deposit of faith. (85-86)

> The Church's Magisterium exercises the authority it holds from Christ to the fullest extent when it defines dogmas, that is, when it proposes truths contained in divine

> Revelation or also when it proposes in a definitive way truths having a necessary connection with them. (88)
>
> The whole body of the faithful. . . cannot err in matters of belief. (92)
>
> [A]ll that has been said about the manner of interpreting Scripture is ultimately subject to the judgment of the Church which exercises the divinely conferred commission and ministry of watching over and interpreting the Word of God. But I would not believe in the Gospel, had not the authority of the Catholic Church already moved me. (119)
>
> The Church's Magisterium, as authentic interpreter of the affirmations of Scripture and Tradition (1008)

The function and purpose of the Magisterium is for the purity and protection of the RCC as seen in the paragraphs below. However, all this is again based on the belief that there was some kind of apostolic succession to certain men, giving them the authority of Christ on earth. Notice the source of their authority is the Apostles from Christ and therefore the RCC believes they are infallible.

> In order to preserve the Church in the purity of the faith handed on by the apostles, Christ who is the Truth willed to confer on her a share in his own infallibility. By a "supernatural sense of faith" the People of God, under the guidance of the Church's living Magisterium, "unfailingly adheres to this faith. (889)
>
> The mission of the Magisterium is linked to the definitive nature of the covenant established by God with his people in Christ. It is this Magisterium's task to preserve God's people from deviations and defections and to guarantee them the objective possibility of professing the true faith without error. Thus, the pastoral duty of the Magisterium is aimed at seeing to it that the People of God abides in the truth that liberates. To fulfill this service, Christ endowed the Church's shepherds with the charism of infallibility in matters of faith and morals. The exercise of this charism takes several forms: (890)

The Roman Pontiff, head of the college of bishops, enjoys this infallibility in virtue of his office, when, as supreme pastor and teacher of all the faithful—who confirms his brethren in the faith he proclaims by a definitive act a doctrine pertaining to faith or morals.... The infallibility promised to the Church is also present in the body of bishops when, together with Peter's successor, they exercise the supreme Magisterium, above all in an Ecumenical Council. When the Church through its supreme Magisterium proposes a doctrine for belief as being divinely revealed, and as the teaching of Christ, the definitions must be adhered to with the obedience of faith. This infallibility extends as far as the deposit of divine Revelation itself. (891)

The Roman Pontiff and the bishops are authentic teachers, that is, teachers endowed with the authority of Christ, who preach the faith to the people entrusted to them, the faith to be believed and put into practice. The ordinary and universal Magisterium of the Pope and the bishops in communion with him teach the faithful the truth to believe, the charity to practice, the beatitude to hope for. (2034)

The Church, the "pillar and bulwark of the truth," has received this solemn command of Christ from the apostles to announce the saving truth. To the Church belongs the right always and everywhere to announce moral principles, including those pertaining to the social order, and to make judgments on any human affairs to the extent that they are required by the fundamental rights of the human person or the salvation of souls. (2036)

Personal conscience and reason should not be set in opposition to the moral law or the Magisterium of the Church. (2039)

The infallibility of the Magisterium of the Pastors extends to all the elements of doctrine, including moral doctrine, without which the saving truths of the faith cannot be preserved, expounded, or observed. (2051)

To summarize the three-fold authority of the RCC, there is Scripture, which is interpreted via the tradition and both are interpreted by the RCC via the Magisterium. In order for people to know the Scriptures they must first be Catholic and then be taught by the Magisterium. It can be pictured as layers, with Scripture at the center. To get to the Scripture you must have the next layer, tradition. However, the tradition requires the Magisterium. The outer most layer is the Catholic congregation who must believe only what the Magisterium teach.

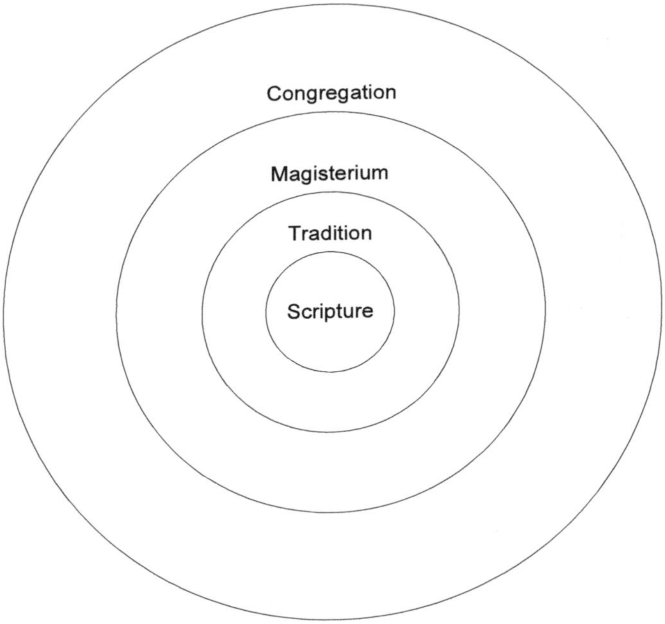

The RCC sets itself up as God's only means of truth on earth, because without the RCC God's Word cannot be understood. They so confuse things that they make the RCC the reason for life, not God. God created all things for His glory. However, the RCC states, "The world was created for the sake of the Church" (760). It is for this reason that some could say that the RCC is church-centered with a church-worship instead of God-centered with a God-worship. The RCC believes it is the center of all God's plans. To be forgiven of sin in the sacrament of penance one must "be faithful to the Magisterium of the Church" (1466).

> The Church is both the means and the goal of God's plan: prefigured in creation, prepared for in the Old Covenant,

> founded by the words and actions of Jesus Christ, fulfilled by his redeeming cross and his Resurrection, the Church has been manifested as the mystery of salvation by the outpouring of the Holy Spirit. She will be perfected in the glory of heaven as the assembly of all the redeemed of the earth. (778)
>
> Christ and his Church thus together make up the "whole Christ". The Church is one with Christ. (765)

God

The RCC "never ceases to proclaim her faith in one only God: Father, Son and Holy Spirit" (152). The RCC believes the "Trinity is One. [They] do not confess three Gods, but one God in three persons … The divine persons do not share the one divinity among themselves but each of them is God whole and entire … The divine persons are really distinct from one another. God is one but not solitary. "Father", "Son", "Holy Spirit" are not simply names designating modalities of the divine being, for they are really distinct from one another" (253-254).

Below are more paragraphs that support the RCC doctrine.

> We must believe in no one but God: the Father, the Son and the Holy Spirit. (178)
>
> [T]he truths of faith professed during Baptism are articulated in terms of their reference to the three persons of the Holy Trinity. And so the Creed is divided into three parts: the first part speaks of the first divine Person and the wonderful work of creation; the next speaks of the second divine Person and the mystery of his redemption of men; the final part speaks of the third divine Person, the origin and source of our sanctification. These three parts are distinct although connected with one another. (189-191)
>
> God is unique; there is only one God: The Christian faith confesses that God is one in nature, substance and essence. (200)

> Jesus himself affirms that God is the one Lord ... At the same time Jesus gives us to understand that he himself is the Lord. To confess that Jesus is Lord is distinctive of Christian faith. This is not contrary to belief in the One God. Nor does believing in the Holy Spirit as Lord and giver of life introduce any division into the One God: We firmly believe and confess without reservation that there is only one true God, eternal infinite (immensus) and unchangeable, incomprehensible, almighty and ineffable, the Father and the Son and the Holy Spirit; three persons indeed, but one essence, substance or nature entirely simple. (202)
>
> Christians are baptized in the name of the Father and of the Son and of the Holy Spirit: not in their names,[55] for there is only one God, the almighty Father, his only Son and the Holy Spirit: the Most Holy Trinity. (233)

Jesus Christ

There is little question that the RCC accepts a Biblical view of the Deity of Jesus Christ. However, since the RCC has devoted much of its theology to the doctrine of Mary and since Mary is tightly tied to her Son, Jesus Christ, Mary will be discussed with her Son.

Deity of Jesus Christ

The RCC clearly believes that Jesus Christ was fully God and fully Man; two natures in one body (464, 468-470, 479-483).

> Jesus Christ is true God and true man, in the unity of his divine person; for this reason he is the one and only mediator between God and men. (480)

The following paragraphs explain this doctrine.

> The Church thus confesses that Jesus is inseparably true God and true man. He is truly the Son of God who, without ceasing to be God and Lord, became a man and our brother (469)

The unique and altogether singular event of the Incarnation of the Son of God does not mean that Jesus Christ is part God and part man, nor does it imply that he is the result of a confused mixture of the divine and the human. He became truly man while remaining truly God. Jesus Christ is true God and true man. (464)

[T]he fifth ecumenical council, at Constantinople in 553, confessed that "there is but one hypostasis [or person], which is our Lord Jesus Christ, one of the Trinity. ... He who was crucified in the flesh, our Lord Jesus Christ, is true God, Lord of glory, and one of the Holy Trinity.(468)

Because human nature was assumed, not absorbed, in the mysterious union of the Incarnation, the Church was led over the course of centuries to confess the full reality of Christ's human soul, with its operations of intellect and will, and of his human body. In parallel fashion, she had to recall on each occasion that Christ's human nature belongs, as his own, to the divine person of the Son of God, who assumed it. Everything that Christ is and does in this nature derives from one of the Trinity. The Son of God therefore communicates to his humanity his own personal mode of existence in the Trinity. In his soul as in his body, Christ thus expresses humanly the divine ways of the Trinity: The Son of God. . . worked with human hands; he thought with a human mind. He acted with a human will, and with a human heart he loved. Born of the Virgin Mary, he has truly been made one of us, like to us in all things except sin. (470)

Christ possesses two wills and two natural operations, divine and human. (475)

At the time appointed by God, the only Son of the Father, the eternal Word, that is, the Word and substantial Image of the Father, became incarnate; without losing his divine nature he has assumed human nature. (479)

Jesus Christ is true God and true man, in the unity of his divine person; for this reason he is the one and only mediator between God and men. (480)

> Jesus Christ possesses two natures, one divine and the other human, not confused, but united in the one person of God's Son. (481)
>
> Christ, being true God and true man, has a human intellect and will, perfectly attuned and subject to his divine intellect and divine will, which he has in common with the Father and the Holy Spirit. (482)
>
> The Incarnation is therefore the mystery of the wonderful union of the divine and human natures in the one person of the Word. (483)

Mary

The emphasis on Mary is unique to the RCC. This doctrine of Mary was developed over time by the RCC.

> *Through the centuries* the Church has become ever more aware that Mary, 'full of grace' through God, was redeemed from the moment of her conception. (491) (emphasis added)

To the point that today the RCC refers to her as, "Mary the all-holy ever-virgin Mother of God" (721). They believe that Mary is the ultimate example of faith (144, 149, 165, 489, 2030); she has become the "new Eve" as Christ is the "new Adam" (411, 511) and that she had a choice in the conception of Jesus (484, 511).

The RCC's position is that Jesus must continue to honor his mother, therefore, intercession to Mary is a first step to talk to Jesus. Furthermore, the theory is that in order for Mary to give birth to God she had to be sinless herself. The flaw in this thinking is that in order for Mary's mother to give birth to a sinless daughter, she too would need to be sinless. However, this theory of Mary's sinlessness causes many flawed doctrines related to Mary from the RCC. They make Mary's birth, life and death special like Jesus'.

They believe that Mary was given special grace at birth so that she could later bear the Christ. Therefore, her life is different because she is the only human to live a sinless life. Then after

Christ's death they believe she took on a special ministry of prayer, because Jesus would listen to her prayer more then anyone else. They then make her death different in that they say she, like Christ, ascended to heaven.

See the paragraphs below that were referenced above:

> The Virgin Mary is [faith's] most perfect embodiment. (144)
>
> Throughout her life and until her last ordeal when Jesus her son died on the cross, Mary's faith never wavered. She never ceased to believe in the fulfillment of God's word. And so the Church venerates in Mary the purest realization of faith. (149)
>
> Mary stands out among the poor and humble of the Lord, who confidently hope for and receive salvation from him. After a long period of waiting the times are fulfilled in her, the exalted Daughter of Sion, and the new plan of salvation is established. (489)
>
> The Christian tradition sees in this passage an announcement of the "New Adam" who, because he "became obedient unto death, even death on a cross", makes amends superabundantly for the disobedience, of Adam.[305] Furthermore many Fathers and Doctors of the Church have seen the woman announced in the "Proto-evangelium" as Mary, the mother of Christ, the "new Eve". Mary benefited first of all and uniquely from Christ's victory over sin: she was preserved from all stain of original sin and by a special grace of God committed no sin of any kind during her whole earthly life (411)

RCC believe Mary had some role in the decision of the conception of Jesus Christ. RCC says she was invited to conceive Christ. However, in the gospels she was told what things would happen, she was not given a choice or invitation.

> Mary was invited to conceive him in whom the whole fullness of deity would dwell bodily. (484)

> The Virgin Mary cooperated through free faith and obedience in human salvation. She uttered her yes in the name of all human nature. By her obedience she became the new Eve, mother of the living. (511)

The paragraphs below show some of the depths that the RCC goes in explaining this doctrine of Mary. These paragraphs show why it is that the RCC see Mary as worthy of almost worship. She is placed as close to being God as a human can get. To the point that in heaven we should look forward to not only seeing Christ but desire to see Mary too.

> What the Catholic faith believes about Mary is based on what it believes about Christ, and what it teaches about Mary illumines in faith in Christ. (487)
>
> [Mary's] spiritual motherhood extends to all men whom indeed [Christ] came to save. (501)
>
> Mary, the all-holy ever-virgin Mother of God, is the masterwork of the mission of the Son and the Spirit in the fullness of time. For the first time in the plan of salvation and because his Spirit had prepared her, the Father found the dwelling place where his Son and his Spirit could dwell among men. In this sense the Church's Tradition has often read the most beautiful texts on wisdom in relation to Mary. Mary is acclaimed and represented in the liturgy as the "Seat of Wisdom." In her, the "wonders of God" that the Spirit was to fulfill in Christ and the Church began to be manifested: (721)
>
> The Holy Spirit prepared Mary by his grace. It was fitting that the mother of him in whom the whole fullness of deity dwells bodily should herself be full of grace. She was, by sheer grace, conceived without sin as the most humble of creatures, the most capable of welcoming the inexpressible gift of the Almighty. It was quite correct for the angel Gabriel to greet her as the Daughter of Zion: Rejoice. It is the thanksgiving of the whole People of God, and thus of the Church, which Mary in her canticle lifts up to the Father in the Holy Spirit while carrying within her the eternal Son. (722)

> In Mary, the Holy Spirit fulfills the plan of the Father's loving goodness. With and through the Holy Spirit, the Virgin conceives and gives birth to the Son of God. By the Holy Spirit's power and her faith, her virginity became uniquely fruitful. (723)
>
> In Mary, the Holy Spirit manifests the Son of the Father, now become the Son of the Virgin. She is the burning bush of the definitive theophany. Filled with the Holy Spirit she makes the Word visible in the humility of his flesh. It is to the poor and the first representatives of the gentiles that she makes him known. (724)
>
> Finally, through Mary, the Holy Spirit begins to bring men, the objects of God's merciful love, into communion with Christ. And the humble are always the first to accept him: shepherds, magi, Simeon and Anna, the bride and groom at Cana, and the first disciples. (725)
>
> At the end of this mission of the Spirit, Mary became the Woman, the new Eve ("mother of the living"), the mother of the whole Christ. As such, she was present with the Twelve, who with one accord devoted themselves to prayer, at the dawn of the "end time" which the Spirit was to inaugurate on the morning of Pentecost with the manifestation of the Church. (726)
>
> We believe that the multitude of those gathered around Jesus and Mary in Paradise forms the Church of heaven. (1053)

Mother of God

Mary is often called the “Mother of God” (469, 493, 495, 508-509, 721, 963, 975, 1014, 1172). The RCC believe that it was Mary’s “faith that enables her to become the mother of the Savior” (506). Due to the teaching that Mary was the mother of God, the RCC believes that she “was enriched by God with gifts appropriate to such a role” (490).

If it was Mary’s faith that enabled her to assume this role and due to this role she was made sinless, it could be said that Mary merited her own sinlessness. So how did Mary start becoming known as the mother of God?

> The Council of Ephesus proclaim in 431 that Mary truly became the Mother of God by the human conception of the Son of God in her womb. (466)

The Council was arguing the Deity of Christ. The phrase "mother of God" was not a reflection on Mary as much as it was a comment on Christ being God. It was not stating that Mary was any different type of human being but that she was chosen to bear not just a man but a man who was God.

> To become the mother of the Saviour, Mary was enriched by God with gifts appropriate to such a role. The angel Gabriel at the moment of the annunciation salutes her as "full of grace". In fact, in order for Mary to be able to give the free assent of her faith to the announcement of her vocation, it was necessary that she be wholly borne by God's grace. (490)

Mother of "The Church"

As great as the ministry of Peter (the Pope) is to the RCC, Mary's ministry is greater, because she is the mother of the RCC (733). Mary has a special ministry to the church as the mother of the church and intercessor to her Son and working with Him in redemption (970).

The following paragraphs explain this doctrine.

> Mary is the symbol and the most perfect realization of the Church. (507)

> Mary goes before us all in the holiness that is the Church's mystery as the bride without spot or wrinkle. This is why the "Maian" dimension of the Church precedes the "Petrine". (773)

> But while in the most Blessed Virgin the Church has already reached that perfection whereby she exists without spot or wrinkle, the faithful still strive to conquer sin and

increase in holiness. And so they turn their eyes to Mary: in her, the Church is already the "all-holy." (829)

[The RCC's] holiness shines in the saints; in Mary [the RCC] is already all-holy. (867)

The Virgin Mary . . . is acknowledged and honored as being truly the Mother of God and of the redeemer.... She is 'clearly the mother of the members of Christ' "Mary, Mother of Christ, Mother of the Church." (963)

Mary's role in the Church is inseparable from her union with Christ and flows directly from it. This union of the mother with the Son in the work of salvation is made manifest from the time of Christ's virginal conception up to his death; Thus the Blessed Virgin advanced in her pilgrimage of faith, and faithfully persevered in her union with her Son unto the cross. There she stood, in keeping with the divine plan, enduring with her only begotten Son the intensity of his suffering, joining herself with his sacrifice in her mother's heart, and lovingly consenting to the immolation of this victim, born of her: (964)

After her Son's Ascension, Mary aided the beginnings of the Church by her prayers. In her association with the apostles and several women, we also see Mary by her prayers imploring the gift of the Spirit, who had already overshadowed her in the Annunciation. (965)

the Virgin Mary is the Church's model of faith and charity. ... she is the exemplary realization of the Church. (967)

she is a mother to us in the order of grace. (968)

This motherhood of Mary in the order of grace continues uninterruptedly from the consent which she loyally gave at the Annunciation and which she sustained without wavering beneath the cross, until the eternal fulfilment of all the elect. Taken up to heaven she did not lay aside this saving office but by her manifold intercession continues to bring us the gifts of eternal salvation .... Therefore the

> Blessed Virgin is invoked in the Church under the titles of Advocate, Helper, Benefactress, and Mediatrix. (969)
>
> "Mary's function as mother of men in no way obscures or diminishes this unique mediation of Christ, but rather shows its power. ... just as the priesthood of Christ is shared in various ways both by his ministers and the faithful, and as the one goodness of God is radiated in different ways among his creatures, so also the unique mediation of the Redeemer does not exclude but rather gives rise to a manifold cooperation which is but a sharing in this one source. (970)
>
> By pronouncing her fiat at the Annunciation and giving her consent to the Incarnation, Mary was already collaborating with the whole work her Son was to accomplish. She is mother wherever he is Savior and head of the Mystical Body. (973)
>
> We believe that the Holy Mother of God, the new Eve, Mother of the Church, continues in heaven to exercise her maternal role on behalf of the members of Christ (975)

All-Holy Sinless One

The RCC teaches that at conception Mary did not have the affects of original sin and was preserved from all stain of sin throughout her life (411, 508).

The following paragraphs explain this doctrine.

> Mary benefited first of all and uniquely from Christ's victory over sin: she was preserved from all stain of original sin and by a special grace of God committed no sin of any kind during her whole earthly life. (411)
>
> To become the mother of the Saviour, Mary was enriched by God with gifts appropriate to such a role. The angel Gabriel at the moment of the annunciation salutes her as "full of grace". In fact, in order for Mary to be able to give the free assent of her faith to the announcement of her

vocation, it was necessary that she be wholly borne by God's grace. (490)

Through the centuries the Church has become ever more aware that Mary, "full of grace" through God, was redeemed from the moment of her conception. That is what the dogma of the Immaculate Conception confesses, as Pope Pius IX proclaimed in 1854: The most Blessed Virgin Mary was, from the first moment of her conception, by a singular grace and privilege of almighty God and by virtue of the merits of Jesus Christ, Saviour of the human race, preserved immune from all stain of original sin. (491)

The splendour of an entirely unique holiness by which Mary is enriched from the first instant of her conception comes wholly from Christ: she is redeemed, in a more exalted fashion, by reason of the merits of her Son. The Father blessed Mary more than any other created person in Christ with every spiritual blessing in the heavenly places and chose her in Christ before the foundation of the world, to be holy and blameless before him in love. (492)

The Fathers of the Eastern tradition call the Mother of God "the All-Holy", and celebrate her as free from any stain of sin, as though fashioned by the Holy Spirit and formed as a new creature. By the grace of God Mary remained free of every personal sin her whole life long. (493)

... without a single sin to restrain her. (494)

... from the first instant of her conception, she was totally preserved from the stain of original sin and she remained pure from all personal sin throughout her life. (508)

She was, by sheer grace, conceived without sin as the most humble of creatures, the most capable of welcoming the inexpressible gift of the Almighty. (722)

But while in the most Blessed Virgin the Church has already reached that perfection whereby she exists without spot or wrinkle, the faithful still strive to conquer sin and

> increase in holiness. And so they turn their eyes to Mary: in her, the Church is already the all-holy. (829)
>
> [T]he Immaculate Virgin, preserved free from all stain of original sin. (966)

Ever-Virgin

The RCC refers to Mary as the "ever-virgin" (469, 507, 721) or "blessed virgin" (964, 971). They believe that Mary remained a virgin even after the birth of Jesus (500). Since she was sinless any more children born to Mary would have been sinless, so God allowed her to give birth only to Jesus Christ.

The thinking of Mary being an ever-virgin lacks the understanding that sin is passed from father (Adam) to children and not from the mother. Also, her virginity has nothing to do with bearing children. She could lose her virginity and still not bear children.

The following paragraphs explain this doctrine.

> The deepening of faith in the virginal motherhood led the Church to confess Mary's real and perpetual virginity even in the act of giving birth to the Son of God made man. In fact, Christ's birth did not diminish his mother's virginal integrity but sanctified it. And so the liturgy of the Church celebrates Mary as Aeiparthenos, the "Ever-virgin". (499)
>
> Against this doctrine the objection is sometimes raised that the Bible mentions brothers and sisters of Jesus. The Church has always understood these passages as not referring to other children of the Virgin Mary. In fact James and Joseph, brothers of Jesus, are the sons of another Mary, a disciple of Christ, whom St. Matthew significantly calls the other Mary. They are close relations of Jesus, according to an Old Testament expression. (500)
>
> Jesus is Mary's only son, but her spiritual motherhood extends to all men whom indeed he came to save. (501)
>
> Mary is a virgin because her virginity is the sign of her faith unadulterated by any doubt, and of her undivided gift of herself to God's will. It is her faith that enables her to

> become the mother of the Saviour: Mary is more blessed because she embraces faith in Christ than because she conceives the flesh of Christ. (506)

> Mary remained a virgin in conceiving her Son, a virgin in giving birth to him, a virgin in carrying him, a virgin in nursing him at her breast, always a virgin. (510)

Sin

The RCC believes that all humans, except Mary, are born with the effects of original sin. However, baptism removes the effects of original sin and leaves the person with a wounded nature or weakness toward sin. The RCC clearly believes that man's will is completely free to choose good or evil; God or sin. The RCC also differentiates between mortal sins (willful acts of deliberate disobedience of a grave nature) and venial sin (willful acts of a lesser nature).

A failure to understand God's purpose in creation causes the RCC to have a wrong view of sin. God's purpose for all of creation was for His glory. However, the RCC believes that "God created everything for man" (358). Therefore, they end up seeing sin from a man-centered view. They see sin as "an offense against reason, truth, and right conscience; it is failure in genuine love for God and neighbor caused by a perverse attachment to certain goods. It wounds the nature of man and injures human solidarity" (1849).

Although they do state that it is an offense against God they immediately follow it up by stating, "Sin sets itself against God's love for us and turns our hearts away from it" (1850). In other words, sin is an offense against God because it set us against the love that God so much wants to show us, because we are such good people and everything was created for man. This view causes them to believe that no man can forget or reject God (29-30). They do not see men as enemies of God.

> But this intimate and vital bond of man to God can be forgotten, overlooked, or even explicitly rejected by man. (29)

> Although man can forget God or reject him, He never ceases to call every man to seek him, so as to find life and happiness. But this search for God demands of man every effort of intellect, a sound will, "an upright heart", as well as the witness of others who teach him to seek God. (30)

> Sin is an act contrary to reason. It wounds man's nature and injures human solidarity. (1872)

> Sin is a personal act. Moreover, we have a responsibility for the sins committed by others when we cooperate in them:
> —by participating directly and voluntarily in them;
> —by ordering, advising, praising, or approving them;
> —by not disclosing or not hindering them when we have an obligation to do so;
> —by protecting evil-doers. (1868)

The RCC sees sin as solely controllable by man's actions therefore habitual sin continues. Where Christianity would see the Holy Spirit involved in working in the heart to change man's thinking about personal sins.

> Sin creates a proclivity to sin; it engenders vice by repetition of the same acts. (1865)

> The repetition of sins—even venial ones—engenders vices, among which are the capital sins. (1876)

The RCC believes that a child of God has one united nature, spiritual and sinful, not two natures in one body.

> The unity of soul and body is so profound that one has to consider the soul to be the "form" of the body: i.e., it is because of its spiritual soul that the body made of matter becomes a living, human body; spirit and matter, in man, are not two natures united, but rather their union forms a single nature. (365)

> The Church teaches that every spiritual soul is created immediately by God—it is not "produced" by the parents—and also that it is immortal: it does not perish when it

> separates from the body at death, and it will be reunited with the body at the final Resurrection. (366)

The follow passages are some descriptions of the RCC distinction and description of mortal sins verses venial sins. Christianity sees sin as sin. All and any sin is an offense against God. The consequences may differ; however, all sins are forgivable by God through the finished work of Christ on the cross, not by the confession or works of repentance.

> Sins can be distinguished according to their objects, as can every human act ... they can be divided into spiritual and carnal sins, or again as sins in thought, word, deed, or omission. (1853)

> Sins are rightly evaluated according to their gravity. The distinction between mortal and venial sin, already evident in Scripture, became part of the tradition of the Church. It is corroborated by human experience. (1854)

> Mortal sin destroys charity in the heart of man by a grave violation of God's law; it turns man away from God, who is his ultimate end and his beatitude, by preferring an inferior good to him. Venial sin allows charity to subsist, even though it offends and wounds it. (1855)

> Mortal sin, by attacking the vital principle within us—that is, charity—necessitates a new initiative of God's mercy and a conversion of heart which is normally accomplished within the setting of the sacrament of reconciliation. (1856)

> For a sin to be mortal, three conditions must together be met: Mortal sin is sin whose object is grave matter and which is also committed with full knowledge and deliberate consent. (1857)

> The gravity of sins is more or less great: murder is graver than theft. One must also take into account who is wronged: violence against parents is in itself graver than violence against a stranger. (1858)

Mortal sin requires full knowledge and complete consent. It presupposes knowledge of the sinful character of the act, of its opposition to God's law. (1859)

Unintentional ignorance can diminish or even remove the imputability of a grave offense. (1860)

Mortal sin is a radical possibility of human freedom, as is love itself. It results in the loss of charity and the privation of sanctifying grace, that is, of the state of grace. If it is not redeemed by repentance and God's forgiveness, it causes exclusion from Christ's kingdom and the eternal death of hell, for our freedom has the power to make choices for ever, with no turning back. However, although we can judge that an act is in itself a grave offense, we must entrust judgment of persons to the justice and mercy of God. (1861)

One commits venial sin when, in a less serious matter, he does not observe the standard prescribed by the moral law, or when he disobeys the moral law in a grave matter, but without full knowledge or without complete consent. (1862)

Venial sin weakens charity; it manifests a disordered affection for created goods; it impedes the soul's progress in the exercise of the virtues and the practice of the moral good; it merits temporal punishment. Deliberate and unrepented venial sin disposes us little by little to commit mortal sin. However venial sin does not set us in direct opposition to the will and friendship of God; it does not break the covenant with God. (1863)

The root of all sins lies in man's heart. The kinds and the gravity of sins are determined principally by their objects. (1873)

To choose deliberately—that is, both knowing it and willing it—something gravely contrary to the divine law and to the ultimate end of man is to commit a mortal sin. This destroys in us the charity without which eternal beatitude is impossible. Unrepented, it brings eternal death. (1874)

> Venial sin constitutes a moral disorder that is reparable by charity, which it allows to subsist in us. (1875)

The RCC view of man and sin affects their view of morality. They start trying to define sins of disobedience by determining willful acts versus ignorant acts. Willful acts of sin are counted against the man and needing some kind of work of repentance, where ignorant acts are not really sin (1859-1860, 1862, 1874).

> Every act directly willed is imputable to its author. (1736)

> An effect can be tolerated without being willed by its agent ... A bad effect is not imputable if it was not willed either as an end or as a means of an action ... For a bad effect to be imputable it must be foreseeable and the agent must have the possibility of avoiding it. (1737)

> Freedom is the power to act or not to act, and so to perform deliberate acts of one's own. Freedom attains perfection in its acts when directed toward God, the sovereign Good. (1744)

> Freedom characterizes properly human acts. It makes the human being responsible for acts of which he is the voluntary agent. His deliberate acts properly belong to him. (1745)

> The imputability or responsibility for an action can be diminished or nullified by ignorance, duress, fear, and other psychological or social factors. (1746)

> The morality of human acts depends on:
> —the object chosen;
> —the end in view or the intention;
> —the circumstances of the action.
> The object, the intention, and the circumstances make up the "sources," or constitutive elements, of the morality of human acts. (1750)

> The object chosen is a good toward which the will deliberately directs itself. It is the matter of a human act. The object chosen morally specifies the act of the will,

insofar as reason recognizes and judges it to be or not to be in conformity with the true good. Objective norms of morality express the rational order of good and evil, attested to by conscience. (1751)

In contrast to the object, the intention resides in the acting subject. Because it lies at the voluntary source of an action and determines it by its end, intention is an element essential to the moral evaluation of an action. The end is the first goal of the intention and indicates the purpose pursued in the action. The intention is a movement of the will toward the end: it is concerned with the goal of the activity. (1752)

The end does not justify the means. Thus the condemnation of an innocent person cannot be justified as a legitimate means of saving the nation. On the other hand, an added bad intention (such as vainglory) makes an act evil that, in and of itself, can be good (such as almsgiving). (1753)

The circumstances, including the consequences, are secondary elements of a moral act. They contribute to increasing or diminishing the moral goodness or evil of human acts (for example, the amount of a theft). They can also diminish or increase the agent's responsibility (such as acting out of a fear of death). Circumstances of themselves cannot change the moral quality of acts themselves; they can make neither good nor right an action that is in itself evil. (1754)

A morally good act requires the goodness of the object, of the end, and of the circumstances together. An evil end corrupts the action, even if the object is good in itself (such as praying and fasting "in order to be seen by men"). The object of the choice can by itself vitiate an act in its entirety. There are some concrete acts—such as fornication—that it is always wrong to choose, because choosing them entails a disorder of the will, that is, a moral evil. (1755)

> It is therefore an error to judge the morality of human acts by considering only the intention that inspires them or the circumstances (environment, social pressure, duress or emergency, etc.) which supply their context. There are acts which, in and of themselves, independently of circumstances and intentions, are always gravely illicit by reason of their object; such as blasphemy and perjury, murder and adultery. One may not do evil so that good may result from it. (1756)
>
> An evil action cannot be justified by reference to a good intention. The end does not justify the means. (1759)
>
> A morally good act requires the goodness of its object, of its end, and of its circumstances together. (1760)
>
> There are concrete acts that it is always wrong to choose, because their choice entails a disorder of the will, i.e., a moral evil. One may not do evil so that good may result from it. (1761)

Original Sin

The RCC believes in original sin, meaning that the sin nature is transmitted from Adam to every human, except Mary (402, 404, 417-418).

The RCC view is for the most part the Biblical as far defined above, with the exception that Mary did have a sin nature. Christianity believes that the sin of Adam was pride not "yielding to tempter". However, the sin of Adam is transmitted to everyone as a state of man, called a sin nature.

> All men are implicated in Adam's sin. (402)
>
> Adam had received original holiness and justice not for himself alone, but for all human nature. By yielding to the tempter, Adam and Eve committed a personal sin, but this sin affected the human nature that they would then transmit in a fallen state. It is a sin which will be transmitted by propagation to all mankind, that is, by the transmission of a human nature deprived of original holiness and justice.

> And that is why original sin is called "sin" only in an analogical sense: it is a sin "contracted" and not "committed"—a state and not an act. (404)

> Adam and Eve transmitted to their descendants human nature wounded by their own first sin and hence deprived of original holiness and justice; this deprivation is called "original sin". (417)

> As a result of original sin, human nature is weakened in its powers, subject to ignorance, suffering and the domination of death, and inclined to sin (this inclination is called "concupiscence"). (418)

Wounded Nature (Weakness toward Sin)

The RCC does not believe that the human nature has been totally corrupted by sin but only wounded and in a weakened state.

> "It is a deprivation of original holiness and justice, but human nature has not been totally corrupted: it is wounded" (405).

They believe that baptism washes away the effects of original sin and leaves the baptized person with a wounded nature that is inclined to sin but not in bondage to sin (405).

The RCC does not understand the extent of sin's affect in the being of man. Their view is that sin is more than just a bad example (Pelagius' view in the fifth century) but not much more. It is viewed for the most part as a bad influence. However, they clearly do not believe that sin has affected the human will to freely choose God (as the next section will discuss).

The RCC's view is that of a reaction to the protestant reformers. The RCC states, "The first Protestant reformers, on the contrary, taught that original sin has radically perverted man and destroyed his freedom; they identified the sin inherited by each man with the tendency to evil" (406). The Reformers taught that the depravity of man means that man's whole being including his will has been affected by original sin and cannot choose God apart from a work of God in the heart of man. The RCC reacts to this by expressing the complete freedom of the will of man.

Below are more paragraphs to support the RCC view of the wounded nature.

> In the historical conditions in which he finds himself, however, man experiences many difficulties in coming to know God by the light of reason alone: Though human reason is, strictly speaking, truly capable by its own natural power and light of attaining to a true and certain knowledge of the one personal God, who watches over and controls the world by his providence, and of the natural law written in our hearts by the Creator; yet there are many obstacles which prevent reason from the effective and fruitful use of this inborn faculty. ... The human mind, in its turn, is hampered in the attaining of such truths, not only by the impact of the senses and the imagination, but also by disordered appetites which are the consequences of original sin. So it happens that men in such matters easily persuade themselves that what they would not like to be true is false or at least doubtful. (37)

> [T]he overwhelming misery which oppresses men and their inclination towards evil . (403)

> It is a deprivation of original holiness and justice, but human nature has not been totally corrupted: it is wounded in the natural powers proper to it, subject to ignorance, suffering and the dominion of death, and inclined to sin—an inclination to evil that is called concupiscence". Baptism, by imparting the life of Christ's grace, erases original sin and turns a man back towards God, but the consequences for nature, weakened and inclined to evil, persist in man and summon him to spiritual battle. (405)

> By our first parents' sin, the devil has acquired a certain domination over man, even though man remains free. Original sin entails captivity under the power of him who thenceforth had the power of death, that is, the devil. Ignorance of the fact that man has a wounded nature

inclined to evil gives rise to serious errors in the areas of education, politics, social action and morals. (407)

This expression can also refer to the negative influence exerted on people by communal situations and social structures that are the fruit of men's sins. (408)

When we made our first profession of faith while receiving the holy Baptism that cleansed us, the forgiveness we received then was so full and complete that there remained in us absolutely nothing left to efface, neither original sin nor offenses committed by our own will, nor was there left any penalty to suffer in order to expiate them.... Yet the grace of Baptism delivers no one from all the weakness of nature. On the contrary, we must still combat the movements of concupiscence that never cease leading us into evil. (978)

Our inclination towards evil ... (979)

The term "flesh" refers to man in his state of weakness and mortality. (990)

Such frailties inherent in life as weakness of character, and so on, as well as an inclination to sin ... (1264)

Conversion to Christ, the new birth of Baptism, the gift of the Holy Spirit and the Body and Blood of Christ received as food have made us "holy and without blemish, just as the Church herself, the Bride of Christ, is "holy and without blemish. Nevertheless the new life received in Christian initiation has not abolished the frailty and weakness of human nature, nor the inclination to sin that tradition calls concupiscence, which remains in the baptized such that with the help of tho grace of Christ they may prove themselves in the struggle of Christian life. This is the struggle of conversion directed toward holiness and eternal life to which the Lord never ceases to call us. (1426)

[S]in also injures and weakens the sinner himself, as well as his relationships with God and neighbor. Absolution takes away sin, but it does not remedy all the disorders sin

> has caused. Raised up from sin, the sinner must still recover his full spiritual health by doing something more to make amends for the sin: he must "make satisfaction for" or "expiate" his sins. (1459)
>
> [Man] still desires the good, but his nature bears the wound of original sin. He is now inclined to evil and subject to error. (1707)
>
> The beatitudes ... invites us to purify our hearts of bad instincts. (1723)

Free Will

The RCC teaches that man's will must be completely free to choose God in order respond to God's call to man (27, 33, 160, 180, 311, 364). The human will was not affected by Adam's act of sin in the garden. The human will is free to make godly choices without the influence of sin.

The RCC believes that man must have remained with a free will after the fall because it is the divine image of God in man. Much of the argument is based on man's ability to reason and intellect. However, Scripture says man should not rest upon his own understanding (reason and intellect).

The issue of freedom of the will refers to the belief that the will is not influenced by any outside influences, i.e. sin. Christianity would believe that the will of man is influenced by sin and captive to sin and therefore is not free.

Below are some more paragraphs to support the RCC view of free will.

> [Man] cannot live fully according to truth unless he freely acknowledges that love and entrusts himself to his creator. (27)
>
> The human person: with his openness to truth and beauty, his sense of moral goodness, his freedom and the voice of his conscience, with his longings for the infinite and for happiness, man questions himself about God's existence. (33)

To be human, man's response to God by faith must be free, and … therefore nobody is to be forced to embrace the faith against his will. The act of faith is of its very nature a free act. (160)

"Believing" is a human act, conscious and free corresponding to the dignity of the human person. (180)

Angels and men, as intelligent and free creatures, have to journey toward their ultimate destinies by their free choice and preferential live. (311)

Through [Christ] [men] are thus brought to their highest perfection and can raise their voice in praise freely given to the Creator. (364)

The affirmations of Sacred Scripture and the teachings of the Church on the subject of hell are a call to the responsibility incumbent upon man to make use of his freedom in view of his eternal destiny. (1036)

God predestines no one to go to hell; for this, a willful turning away from God (a mortal sin) is necessary, and persistence in it until the end. (1037)

It is essential to a human being freely to direct himself to this fulfillment … (1700)

By free will, he is capable of directing himself toward his true good. (1704)

By virtue of his soul and his spiritual powers of intellect and will, man is endowed with freedom, an outstanding manifestation of the divine image. (1705)

[Man] still desires the good, but his nature bears the wound of original sin. He is now inclined to evil and subject to error. (1707)

Endowed with a spiritual soul, with intellect and with free will ,,, (1711)

In man, true freedom is an outstanding manifestation of the divine image. (1712)

Man, having been wounded in his nature by original sin, is subject to error and inclined to evil in exercising his freedom. (1714)

God created man a rational being, conferring on him the dignity of a person who can initiate and control his own actions. "God willed that man should be 'left in the hand of his own counsel,' so that he might of his own accord seek his Creator and freely attain his full and blessed perfection by cleaving to him."[26]
Man is rational and therefore like God; he is created with free will and is master over his acts. (1730)

Freedom is the power, rooted in reason and will, to act or not to act, to do this or that, and so to perform deliberate actions on one's own responsibility. By free will one shapes one's own life. Human freedom is a force for growth and maturity in truth and goodness; it attains its perfection when directed toward God, our beatitude. (1731)

As long as freedom has not bound itself definitively to its ultimate good which is God, there is the possibility of choosing between good and evil, and thus of growing in perfection or of failing and sinning. This freedom characterizes properly human acts. It is the basis of praise or blame, merit or reproach. (1732)

The more one does what is good, the freer one becomes. There is no true freedom except in the service of what is good and just. The choice to disobey and do evil is an abuse of freedom and leads to the slavery of sin. (1733)

Freedom makes man responsible for his acts to the extent that they are voluntary. Progress in virtue, knowledge of the good, and ascesis enhance the mastery of the will over its acts. (1734)

Freedom is exercised in relationships between human beings. Every human person, created in the image of God, has the natural right to be recognized as a free and responsible being. (1738)

Freedom and sin. Man's freedom is limited and fallible. In fact, man failed. He freely sinned. By refusing God's plan of love, he deceived himself and became a slave to sin. This first alienation engendered a multitude of others. From its outset, human history attests the wretchedness and oppression born of the human heart in consequence of the abuse of freedom. (1739)

Threats to freedom. The exercise of freedom does not imply a right to say or do everything. It is false to maintain that man, the subject of this freedom, is an individual who is fully self-sufficient and whose finality is the satisfaction of his own interests in the enjoyment of earthly goods. (1740)

God willed that man should be left in the hand of his own counsel, so that he might of his own accord seek his creator and freely attain his full and blessed perfection by cleaving to him. (1743)

Freedom is the power to act or not to act, and so to perform deliberate acts of one's own. Freedom attains perfection in its acts when directed toward God, the sovereign Good. (1744)

Freedom characterizes properly human acts. It makes the human being responsible for acts of which he is the voluntary agent. His deliberate acts properly belong to him. (1745)

The imputability or responsibility for an action can be diminished or nullified by ignorance, duress, fear, and other psychological or social factors. (1746)

The right to the exercise of freedom, especially in religious and moral matters, is an inalienable requirement of the dignity of man. But the exercise of freedom does not entail the putative right to say or do anything. (1747)

Freedom makes man a moral subject. When he acts deliberately, man is, so to speak, the father of his acts. Human acts, that is, acts that are freely chosen in consequence of a judgment of conscience, can be morally evaluated. They are either good or evil. (1749)

By faith man freely commits his entire self to God. (1814)

Mortal sin is a radical possibility of human freedom, as is love itself. (1861)

Justification establishes cooperation between God's grace and man's freedom. On man's part it is expressed by the assent of faith to the Word of God, which invites him to conversion, and in the cooperation of charity with the prompting of the Holy Spirit who precedes and preserves his assent. (1993)

God's free initiative demands man's free response, for God has created man in his image by conferring on him, along with freedom, the power to know him and love him. The soul only enters freely into the communion of love. (2002)

The merit of man before God in the Christian life arises from the fact that God has freely chosen to associate man with the work of his grace. The fatherly action of God is first on his own initiative, and then follows man's free acting through his collaboration, so that the merit of good works is to be attributed in the first place to the grace of God, then to the faithful. (2008)

The divine initiative in the work of grace precedes, prepares, and elicits the free response of man. Grace responds to the deepest yearnings of human freedom, calls freedom to cooperate with it, and perfects freedom. (2022)

The fifth precept ("You shall observe the prescribed days of fasting and abstinence.") ensures the times of ascesis and penance which prepare us for the liturgical feasts; they help us acquire mastery over our instincts and freedom of heart.(2043)

Salvation

The RCC believes that there are two elements necessary for justification before God (i.e. salvation): faith and works. This was the issue during the reformation when the reformers argued that salvation was by "faith alone" and not by works. The RCC believes both are required and that God dispenses salvation through the "church" and Mary.

As discussed above in the section on authority, the RCC make a direct tie between the authorities of the RCC and salvation (95). Since they believe that it is our choice that saves us then it makes sense that they also believe that our sin can lose us (162). So when they discuss other religions they talk about salvation (kind of) through fearing or acknowledging God (841-843). Although it is not clear if this salvation is the reconciling of man to God or just a drawing toward the RCC or salvation after a time in purgatory. They state anyone who fears God will be saved (781). However, the demons fear God and they are not saved? Therefore, salvation must require something other than just a fear of God.

Below are some more paragraphs to support the RCC view of salvation.

> "It is clear therefore that, in the supremely wise arrangement of God, sacred Tradition, Sacred Scripture and the Magisterium of the Church are so connected and associated that one of them cannot stand without the others. Working together, each in its own way, under the action of the one Holy Spirit, they all contribute effectively to the salvation of souls." (95)

> Faith is an entirely free gift that God makes to man. We can lose this priceless gift, ... To live, grow and persevere in the faith until the end we must nourish it with the word of God; we must beg the Lord to increase our faith; it must be working through charity, abounding in hope, and rooted in the faith of the Church. (162)

> Mary stands out among the poor and humble of the Lord, who confidently hope for and receive salvation from him. After a long period of waiting the times are fulfilled in her,

> the exalted Daughter of Sion, and the new plan of salvation is established. (489)
>
> At all times and in every race, anyone who fears God and does what is right has been acceptable to him. He has, however, willed to make men holy and save them, not as individuals without any bond or link between them, but rather to make them into a people who might acknowledge him and serve him in holiness. (781)
>
> The Church's relationship with the Muslims. The plan of salvation also includes those who acknowledge the Creator, in the first place amongst whom are the Muslims; these profess to hold the faith of Abraham, and together with us they adore the one, merciful God, mankind's judge on the last day. (841)
>
> The Catholic Church recognizes in other religions that search, among shadows and images, for the God who is unknown yet near since he gives life and breath and all things and wants all men to be saved. Thus, the Church considers all goodness and truth found in these religions as a preparation for the Gospel and given by him who enlightens all men that they may at length have life. (843)

Faith

The RCC clearly believes that "faith is man's response to God" (26) and "faith is necessary for salvation" (183). It is something that is obtained by man and can be lost by man (162). It is most often connected with baptism (782, 784, 804, 846, 866, 977, 1226) and works (1815-1816, 2037).

The RCC view of faith is a gift of God but an act of man. The gift of God is the inner workings of the Holy Spirit that allows man to freely choose. Confused? Below are some paragraphs to support the RCC view of faith to help define faith and its purpose in salvation.

> By his Revelation, the invisible God, from the fullness of his love, addresses men as his friends, and moves among them, in order to invite and receive them into his own

company. The adequate response to this invitation is faith. (142)

By faith, man completely submits his intellect and his will to God. With his whole being man gives his assent to God the revealer. Sacred Scripture calls this human response to God, the author of revelation, "the obedience of faith". (143)

To obey ... in faith is to submit freely to the word that has been heard, because its truth is guaranteed by God, who is Truth itself. ... The Virgin Mary is its most perfect embodiment. (144)

Faith is first of all a personal adherence of man to God. At the same time, and inseparably, it is a free assent to the whole truth that God has revealed. (150)

Faith is a gift of God, a supernatural virtue infused by him. Before this faith can be exercised, man must have the grace of God to move and assist him; he must have the interior helps of the Holy Spirit, who moves the heart and converts it to God, who opens the eyes of the mind and 'makes it easy for all to accept and believe the truth. (153)

Believing is possible only by grace and the interior helps of the Holy Spirit. But it is no less true that believing is an authentically human act. Trusting in God and cleaving to the truths he has revealed is contrary neither to human freedom nor to human reason. Even in human relations it is not contrary to our dignity to believe what other persons tell us about themselves and their intentions, or to trust their promises. (154)

In faith, the human intellect and will co-operate with divine grace: Believing is an act of the intellect assenting to the divine truth by command of the will moved by God through grace. (155)

What moves us to believe is not the fact that revealed truths appear as true and intelligible in the light of our natural reason: ... So "that the submission of our faith

> might nevertheless be in accordance with reason, God willed that external proofs of his Revelation should be joined to the internal helps of the Holy Spirit. (156)
>
> Since the same God who reveals mysteries and infuses faith has bestowed the light of reason on the human mind, God cannot deny himself, nor can truth ever contradict truth. (159)
>
> Faith is an entirely free gift that God makes to man. We can lose this priceless gift. (162)
>
> Faith is a personal act—the free response of the human person to the initiative of God who reveals himself. But faith is not an isolated act. No one can believe alone, just as no one can live alone.
> You have not given yourself faith as you have not given yourself life. The believer has received faith from others and should hand it on to others. (166)
>
> Faith is a personal adherence of the whole man to God who reveals himself. It involves an assent of the intellect and will to the self-revelation God has made through his deeds and words. (176)
>
> Faith is a supernatural gift from God. In order to believe, man needs the interior helps of the Holy Spirit. (179)
>
> By faith man freely commits his entire self to God. (1814)

The RCC make a close connection between faith and baptism, as will be discussed below. The following paragraphs reveal this connection.

> One becomes a member of this people not by a physical birth, but by being born anew, a birth of water and the Spirit, that is, by faith in Christ, and Baptism. (782)
>
> On entering the People of God through faith and Baptism. (784)
>
> One enters into the People of God by faith and Baptism. (804)

> [T]he necessity of faith and Baptism … (846)
>
> The Church is one: she acknowledges one Lord, confesses one faith, is born of one Baptism. (866)
>
> Our Lord tied the forgiveness of sins to faith and Baptism. (977)
>
> Always, Baptism is seen as connected with faith. (1226)
>
> … the response of faith, which is inseparable from Baptism. Indeed Baptism is "the sacrament of faith" in a particular way, since it is the sacrament entry into the life of faith. (1236)
>
> Uniting us by faith and Baptism … (2017)
>
> … so that all men may attain salvation through faith, Baptism and the observance of the Commandments. (2068)

The RCC also ties faith to saving works.

> The gift of faith remains in one who has not sinned against it. But faith apart from works is dead: when it is deprived of hope and love, faith does not fully unite the believer to Christ and does not make him a living member of his Body. (1815)
>
> Service of and witness to the faith are necessary for salvation. (1816)
>
> Faith and the practice of the Gospel provide each person with an experience of life "in Christ". (2037)

The object of the person's faith is not just Christ but also the RCC.

> … faith in the forgiveness of sins not only with faith in the Holy Spirit, but also with faith in the Church. (976)

Works

The RCC teaches that men can merit grace for their own salvation (546, 781, 2001, 2008) and others (2027). These works of grace are found in the liturgy and the sacraments.

This is coupled with the teachings of the freedom of man and the choice of faith that starts the salvation process but a man must do good works to remain saved (and avoid purgatory). See the paragraphs below for more support on the RCC view of works necessary for salvation.

> Words are not enough; deeds are required. (546)
>
> Even though incorporated into the Church, one who does not however persevere in charity is not saved. (837)
>
> Those who obey the prompting of the Spirit of truth are already on the way of salvation. (851)
>
> The intercession of the saints. Being more closely united to Christ, those who dwell in heaven fix the whole Church more firmly in holiness.... They do not cease to intercede with the Father for us, as they proffer the merits which they acquired on earth through the one mediator between God and men, Christ Jesus.... So by their fraternal concern is our weakness greatly helped. (956)
>
> Who will rise? All the dead will rise, "those who have done good, to the resurrection of life, and those who have done evil, to the resurrection of judgment." (998)
>
> In this way they attained their own salvation and at the same time cooperated in saving their brothers in the unity of the Mystical Body. (1477)
>
> ... it shows the importance of moral decisions for our salvation. (1696)
>
> The gift of faith remains in one who has not sinned against it. But faith apart from works is dead: when it is deprived of hope and love, faith does not fully unite the believer to

Christ and does not make him a living member of his Body. (1815)

Indeed we also work, but we are only collaborating with God who works. (2001)

grace also includes the gifts that the Spirit grants us to associate us with his work, to enable us to collaborate in the salvation of others and in the growth of the Body of Christ, the Church. There are sacramental graces, gifts proper to the different sacraments. (2003)

The merit of man before God in the Christian life arises from the fact that God has freely chosen to associate man with the work of his grace. The fatherly action of God is first on his own initiative, and then follows man's free acting through his collaboration, so that the merit of good works is to be attributed in the first place to the grace of God, then to the faithful. Man's merit, moreover, itself is due to God, for his good actions proceed in Christ, from the predispositions and assistance given by the Holy Spirit. (2008)

merits of our good works are gifts of the divine goodness. Grace has gone before us; now we are given what is due.... Our merits are God's gifts.(2009)

we can then merit for ourselves and for others the graces needed for our sanctification, for the increase of grace and charity, and for the attainment of eternal life. Even temporal goods like health and friendship can be merited in accordance with God's wisdom. (2010)

We can have merit in God's sight only because of God's free plan to associate man with the work of his grace. Merit is to be ascribed in the first place to the grace of God, and secondly to man's collaboration. Man's merit is due to God. (2025)

Moved by the Holy Spirit, we can merit for ourselves and for others all the graces needed to attain eternal life, as well as necessary temporal goods. (2027)

> The Council of Trent teaches that the Ten Commandments are obligatory for Christians and that the justified man is still bound to keep them; the Second Vatican Council confirms: "The bishops, successors of the apostles, receive from the Lord . . . the mission of teaching all peoples, and of preaching the Gospel to every creature, so that all men may attain salvation through faith, Baptism and the observance of the Commandments. (2068)

> What good deed must I do, to have eternal life?—If you would enter into life, keep the commandments. (2075)

Liturgy

The RCC teaches that “Christ manifests, makes present, and communicates his work of salvation through the liturgy of his Church” (1076). The liturgy is the order of worship, sacraments and prayers.

The liturgy often requires the use of special words to be spoken at specific times, i.e. during the sacramental services, etc. The RCC believes that the liturgy, itself, communicates salvation.

> ... in the sacramental liturgy, through its words and symbols, in which the Holy Spirit puts us into communion with Christ; (688)

> In the Church's liturgy the divine blessing is fully revealed and communicated. (1082)

> In the liturgy and the celebration of the sacraments, prayer and teaching are conjoined with the grace of Christ to enlighten and nourish Christian activity. (2031)

> The moral life is a spiritual worship. Christian activity finds its nourishment in the liturgy and the celebration of the sacraments. (2047)

Sacraments

A sacrament is the “visible sign of the hidden reality of salvation” (744). The RCC believes that “they are efficacious” (1127) and “necessary for salvation” (1131).

There are seven sacraments:

1. Baptism

2. Confirmation

3. Eucharist

4. Penance

5. Anointing of the Sick

6. Holy Orders

7. Matrimony (1113)

The sacramental system is the central theme of the RCC. Sacraments are used to unify the RCC (815). The RCC believes that other churches may be close to salvation in Christ, but without the sacraments, properly administered by the apostolic succession, they can never reach their goal. It is in the sacramental system that the RCC dispenses salvation.

> —in the sacramental liturgy, through its words and symbols, in which the Holy Spirit puts us into communion with Christ. (688)

> the term sacramentum emphasizes the visible sign of the hidden reality of salvation which was indicated by the term mystenum. ... The saving work of his holy and sanctifying humanity is the sacrament of salvation, which is revealed and active in the Church's sacraments ... The seven sacraments are the signs and instruments by which the Holy Spirit spreads the grace of Christ the head throughout the Church which is his Body. The Church, then, both contains and communicates the invisible grace she signifies. It is in this analogical sense, that the Church is called a "sacrament." (774)

> The Church in this world is the sacrament of salvation, the sign and the instrument of the communion of God and men. (780)

... through the sacraments, are united in a hidden and real way to Christ in his Passion and glorification. (790)

The ministry in which Christ's emissaries do and give by God's grace what they cannot do and give by their own powers, is called a "sacrament" by the Church's tradition. Indeed, the ministry of the Church is conferred by a special sacrament. (875)

Therefore, the riches of Christ are communicated to all the members, through the sacraments. (947)

Communion of the sacraments. The fruit of all the sacraments belongs to all the faithful. All the sacraments are sacred links uniting the faithful with one another and binding them to Jesus Christ. (950)

In the forgiveness of sins, both priests and sacraments are instruments which our Lord Jesus Christ, the only author and liberal giver of salvation, wills to use in order to efface our sins and give us the grace of justification. (987)

Christ now acts through the sacraments he instituted to communicate his grace. The sacraments are perceptible signs (words and actions) accessible to our human nature. (1084)

Sacraments are "powers that comes forth" from the Body of Christ, which is ever-living and life-giving. They are actions of the Holy Spirit at work in his Body, the Church. They are "the masterworks of God" in the new and everlasting covenant. (1116)

The sacraments are "of the Church" in the double sense that they are "by her" and "for her." They are "by the Church," for she is the sacrament of Christ's action at work in her through the mission of the Holy Spirit. They are "for the Church" in the sense that the sacraments make the Church, since they manifest and communicate to men, above all in the Eucharist, the mystery of communion with the God who is love, One in three persons. (1118)

> The three sacraments of Baptism, Confirmation, and Holy Orders confer, in addition to grace, a sacramental character or "seal" by which the Christian shares in Christ's priesthood and is made a member of the Church according to different states and functions. (1121)
>
> The purpose of the sacraments is to sanctify men, to build up the Body of Christ and, finally, to give worship to God. Because they are signs they also instruct. They not only presuppose faith, but by words and objects they also nourish, strengthen, and express it. That is why they are called 'sacraments of faith. (1123)
>
> the liturgy, above all that of the sacraments, there is an immutable part, a part that is divinely instituted and of which the Church is the guardian, and parts that can be changed, which the Church has the power and on occasion also the duty to adapt to the cultures of recently evangelized peoples. (1205)
>
> What faith confesses, the sacraments communicate: by the sacraments of rebirth, Christians have become children of God. (1692)

1. Baptism

The RCC believes that baptism is necessary for salvation (846) and is efficacious (694, 1306).

> "... the necessity of Baptism for salvation. The Lord himself affirms that Baptism is necessary for salvation. ... Baptism is necessary for salvation ... The Church does not know of any means other than Baptism that assures entry into eternal beatitude; ...God has bound salvation to the sacrament of Baptism" (1256-1257)

When the RCC talks about salvation through faith it is most often linked with baptism (14, 172, 403, 782, 784, 818, 846, 977, 1226, 1236, 1253-1254, 1271, 2017, 2068). The RCC view of baptism is that it washes away the affects of original sin (978, 1263, 1279) and provides the forgiveness of past sins (978, 1263, 1486, 1999).

References to baptism and faith (14, 172, 403, 782, 784, 818, 846, 977, 1226, 1236, 1253-1254, 1271, 2017, 2068).

> The Church has constantly confessed this one faith, received from the one Lord, transmitted by one Baptism. (172)

References to justification by baptism (1987, 1992, 2020).

Baptism removes original sin (978, 1263, 1279).

> Baptism, by imparting the life of Christ's grace, erases original sin and turns a man back towards God, but the consequences for nature, weakened and inclined to evil, persist in man and summon him to spiritual battle. (405)

References to the forgiveness of sin by baptism (976-979, 981, 985, 1213, 1237, 1262, 1265, 1279, 1299, 1434, 2042).

> When we made our first profession of faith while receiving the holy Baptism that cleansed us, the forgiveness we received then was so full and complete that there remained in us absolutely nothing left to efface, neither original sin nor offenses committed by our own will, nor was there left any penalty to suffer in order to expiate them.... Yet the grace of Baptism delivers no one from all the weakness of nature. (978)

> By Baptism all sins are forgiven, original sin and all personal sins, as well as all punishment for sin. (1263)

> The forgiveness of sins committed after Baptism is conferred by a particular sacrament called the sacrament of conversion, confession, penance, or reconciliation. (1486)

> grace of Christ is the gratuitous gift that God makes to us of his own life, infused by the Holy Spirit into our soul to heal it of sin and to sanctify it. It is the sanctifying or deifying grace received in Baptism. (1999)

References to salvation (new life) by baptism (168, 1212, 1219, 1250, 1262, 1277, 1279, 1426, 2042).

> Baptism, since after the invocation of the Holy Spirit it becomes the efficacious sacramental sign of new birth. (694)

> "Baptism is certainly valid and efficacious." (1306)

> the necessity of faith and Baptism, and thereby affirmed at the same time the necessity of the Church which men enter through Baptism as through a door. Hence they could not be saved who, knowing that the Catholic Church was founded as necessary by God through Christ, would refuse either to enter it or to remain in it. (846)

> the washing of regeneration and renewal by the Holy Spirit, for it signifies and actually brings about the birth of water and the Spirit without which no one can enter the kingdom of God. (1215)

> Baptism is the principal place for the first and fundamental conversion. It is by faith in the Gospel and by Baptism that one renounces evil and gains salvation, that is, the forgiveness of all sins and the gift of new life. (1427)

Baptism somehow marks the person with an eternal mark.

> Incorporated into Christ by Baptism, the person baptized is configured to Christ. Baptism seals the Christian with the indelible spiritual mark (character) of his belonging to Christ. No sin can erase this mark, even if sin prevents Baptism from bearing the fruits of salvation. Given once for all, Baptism cannot be repeated. (1272)

Penance

The RCC teaches that they have the power (1442, 1495), by God, to forgive sins committed after baptism (980, 1436, 14591486), in the sacrament of penance. They believe that penance is as necessary for salvation as baptism (980).

Penance has the power to forgive sins committed after baptism.

> The sacrament of Penance is a whole consisting in three actions of the penitent and the priest's absolution. The

penitent's acts are repentance, confession or disclosure of sins to the priest, and the intention to make reparation and do works of reparation. (1491)

It is through the sacrament of Penance that the baptized can be reconciled with God and with the Church: Penance has rightly been called by the holy Fathers "a laborious kind of baptism." This sacrament of Penance is necessary for salvation for those who have fallen after Baptism, just as Baptism is necessary for salvation for those who have not yet been reborn. (980)

It is called the sacrament of forgiveness, since by the priest's sacramental absolution God grants the penitent pardon and peace. It is called the sacrament of Reconciliation, because it imparts to the sinner the life of God who reconciles. (1424)

[Penance] is a remedy to free us from our daily faults and to preserve us from mortal sins. (1436)

Christ instituted the sacrament of Penance for all sinful members of his Church: above all for those who, since Baptism, have fallen into grave sin, and have thus lost their baptismal grace and wounded ecclesial communion. (1446)

But sin also injures and weakens the sinner himself, as well as his relationships with God and neighbor. Absolution takes away sin, but it does not remedy all the disorders sin has caused. Raised up from sin, the sinner must still recover his full spiritual health by doing something more to make amends for the sin: he must "make satisfaction for" or "expiate" his sins. This satisfaction is also called "penance." (1459)

Grave sin deprives us of communion with God and therefore makes us incapable of eternal life, the privation of which is called the "eternal punishment" of sin. (1472)

In the communion of saints, a perennial link of charity exists between the faithful who have already reached their

> heavenly home, those who are expiating their sins in purgatory and those who are still pilgrims on earth. (1475)
>
> The forgiveness of sins committed after Baptism is conferred by a particular sacrament called the sacrament of conversion, confession, penance, or reconciliation. (1486)

Penance is necessary to reconcile man back to God, but that is not enough for the RCC. The reason they believe that the RCC must have the power of absolution (1442, 1495) is to reconcile the sinner to the church (1444-1445, 1484). The power of the RCC to forgive sins will be discussed more in the next section on the church as the dispenser of salvation.

> Christ has willed that in her prayer and life and action his whole Church should be the sign and instrument of the forgiveness and reconciliation that he acquired for us at the price of his blood. But he entrusted the exercise of the power of absolution to the apostolic ministry which he charged with the "ministry of reconciliation." (1442)
>
> In imparting to his apostles his own power to forgive sins the Lord also gives them the authority to reconcile sinners with the Church. ... The office of binding and loosing which was given to Peter was also assigned to the college of the apostles united to its head. (1444)
>
> Reconciliation with the Church is inseparable from reconciliation with God. (1445)
>
> This sacrament reconciles us with the Church. (1469)
>
> The Church, who through the bishop and his priests forgives sins in the name of Jesus Christ and determines the manner of satisfaction, also prays for the sinner and does penance with him. (1448)
>
> Such contrition remits venial sins; it also obtains forgiveness of mortal sins if it includes the firm resolution to have recourse to sacramental confession as soon as possible. (1452)

> By itself however, imperfect contrition cannot obtain the forgiveness of grave sins, but it disposes one to obtain forgiveness in the sacrament of Penance. (1453)

> Confession to a priest is an essential part of the sacrament of Penance: All mortal sins of which penitents after a diligent self-examination are conscious must be recounted by them in confession, even if they are most secret and have been committed against the last two precepts of the Decalogue; for these sins sometimes wound the soul more grievously and are more dangerous than those which are committed openly. When Christ's faithful strive to confess all the sins that they can remember, they undoubtedly place all of them before the divine mercy for pardon. But those who fail to do so and knowingly withhold some, place nothing before the divine goodness for remission through the mediation of the priest, for if the sick person is too ashamed to show his wound to the doctor, the medicine cannot heal what it does not know. (1456)

> Since Christ entrusted to his apostles the ministry of reconciliation, bishops who are their successors, and priests, the bishops' collaborators, continue to exercise this ministry. Indeed bishops and priests, by virtue of the sacrament of Holy Orders, have the power to forgive all sins. (1461)

Notice in the following paragraph that the RCC admits that they have changed the sacrament of penance from public to private. This is an attempt to reconcile their different views of this doctrine over the years. It was supposedly handed down from God that penance needed to be public for the forgiveness of sins but now the RCC can change God's plan. This change was historically due to a change for politics not religion. This is an example of where the RCC adjusts its doctrine to culture.

> Over the centuries the concrete form in which the Church has exercised this power received from the Lord has varied considerably. During the first centuries the reconciliation of Christians who had committed particularly grave sins after their Baptism (for example, idolatry, murder, or adultery) was tied to a very rigorous discipline, according to which

> penitents had to do public penance for their sins, often for years, before receiving reconciliation. To this "order of penitents" (which concerned only certain grave sins), one was only rarely admitted and in certain regions only once in a lifetime. During the seventh century Irish missionaries, inspired by the Eastern monastic tradition, took to continental Europe the "private" practice of penance, which does not require public and prolonged completion of penitential works before reconciliation with the Church. From that time on, the sacrament has been performed in secret between penitent and priest. This new practice envisioned the possibility of repetition and so opened the way to a regular frequenting of this sacrament. It allowed the forgiveness of grave sins and venial sins to be integrated into one sacramental celebration. In its main lines this is the form of penance that the Church has practiced down to our day. (1447)

Below is the RCC definition of indulgences.

> An indulgence is a remission before God of the temporal punishment due to sins whose guilt has already been forgiven, which the faithful Christian who is duly disposed gains under certain prescribed conditions through the action of the Church which, as the minister of redemption, dispenses and applies with authority the treasury of the satisfactions of Christ and the saints. An indulgence is partial or plenary according as it removes either part or all of the temporal punishment due to sin. Indulgences may be applied to the living or the dead. (1471)

> An indulgence is obtained through the Church who, by virtue of the power of binding and loosing granted her by Christ Jesus, intervenes in favor of individual Christians and opens for them the treasury of the merits of Christ and the saints to obtain from the Father of mercies the remission of the temporal punishments due for their sins. (1478)

The Church as Dispenser

The RCC believes that Christ, through apostolic succession, has been given the power of salvation, to forgive sins (1442, 1444). People in churches outside of the RCC can be on their "way of salvation", but the RCC "must go out and meet their desire" (851). The many ways or means of this salvation dispensed via the RCC are through the sacraments and liturgy (875, 979).

The RCC has a necessary role in salvation. Salvation is not obtained without the RCC. The reason for this is that the RCC believes that Christ has entrusted only the RCC to dispense salvation to men. The paragraphs below will support this doctrine.

> It is the Church that believes first, and so bears, nourishes, and sustains my faith. ... It is through the Church that we receive faith and new life in Christ by Baptism. (168)

> Salvation comes from God alone; but because we receive the life of faith through the Church, she is our mother. (169)

> the faith that we have received from the Church. (175)

> the whole Church which transmits the faith to us and in whose midst we believe. (197)

> The power to "bind and loose" connotes the authority to absolve sins, to pronounce doctrinal judgements, and to make disciplinary decisions in the Church. Jesus entrusted this authority to the Church through the ministry of the apostles and in particular through the ministry of Peter, the only one to whom he specifically entrusted the keys of the kingdom. (553)

> For it is through Christ's Catholic Church alone, which is the universal help toward salvation, that the fullness of the means of salvation can be obtained. (816)

> Furthermore, many elements of sanctification and of truth are found outside the visible confines of the Catholic Church: the written Word of God; the life of grace; faith, hope, and charity, with the other interior gifts of the Holy

Spirit, as well as visible elements. Christ's Spirit uses these Churches and ecclesial communities as means of salvation, whose power derives from the fullness of grace and truth that Christ has entrusted to the Catholic Church. (819)

It is in the Church that the fullness of the means of salvation has been deposited. It is in her that by the grace of God we acquire holiness. (824)

Fully incorporated into the society of the Church are those who, possessing the Spirit of Christ, accept all the means of salvation given to the Church together with her entire organization, and who—by the bonds constituted by the profession of faith, the sacraments, ecclesiastical government, and communion—are joined in the visible structure of the Church of Christ, who rules her through the Supreme Pontiff and the bishops. Even though incorporated into the Church, one who does not however persevere in charity is not saved. He remains indeed in the bosom of the Church, but 'in body' not 'in heart. (837)

The Church is the place where humanity must rediscover its unity and salvation. (845)

Outside the Church there is no salvation ... the necessity of the Church which men enter through Baptism as through a door. Hence they could not be saved who, knowing that the Catholic Church was founded as necessary by God through Christ, would refuse either to enter it or to remain in it. (846)

Those who obey the prompting of the Spirit of truth are already on the way of salvation. But the Church, to whom this truth has been entrusted, must go out to meet their desire, so as to bring them the truth. Because she believes in God's universal plan of salvation, the Church must be missionary. (851)

The apostles and their successors carry out this "ministry of reconciliation," not only by announcing to men God's forgiveness merited for us by Christ, and calling them to conversion and faith; but also by communicating to them the forgiveness of sins in Baptism, and reconciling them with God and with the Church through the power of the keys, received from Christ: [The Church] has received the keys of the Kingdom of heaven so that, in her, sins may be forgiven through Christ's blood and the Holy Spirit's action. In this Church, the soul dead through sin comes back to life in order to live with Christ, whose grace has saved us. (981)

There is no offense, however serious, that the Church cannot forgive. (982)

Christ's gift to his Church: the mission and the power to forgive sins through the ministry of the apostles and their successors: ... Were there no forgiveness of sins in the Church, there would be no hope of life to come or eternal liberation. Let us thank God who has given his Church such a gift. (983)

By Christ's will, the Church possesses the power to forgive the sins of the baptized and exercises it through bishops and priests normally in the sacrament of Penance. (986)

Christian liturgy not only recalls the events that save us but actualizes them, makes them present. (1104)

Reborn as sons of God, [the baptized] must profess before men the faith they have received from God through the Church. (1270)

Only priests who have received the faculty of absolving from the authority of the Church can forgive sins in the name of Christ. (1495)

Salvation dispensed through the RCC via the sacraments.

No one can bestow grace on himself; it must be given and offered. ... The ministry in which Christ's emissaries do and give by God's grace what they cannot do and give by their own powers, is called a "sacrament" by the Church's

> tradition. Indeed, the ministry of the Church is conferred by a special sacrament. (875)
>
> If the Church has the power to forgive sins, then Baptism cannot be her only means of using the keys of the Kingdom of heaven received from Jesus Christ. The Church must be able to forgive all penitents their offenses, even if they should sin until the last moment of their lives. (979)

Mary as Dispenser

If the RCC through the succession of Peter can dispense salvation, how much more can Mary? Since her ministry is greater than Peter's (733). Mary's current ministry is to intercede for those on earth and bestow upon them certain grace in the work of salvation (725, 969, 970, 1014).

[Mary] is inseparably linked with the saving work of her Son. (1172)

As discussed above Mary is held to an unbiblical place of greatness and authority in the RCC. This doctrine is all based on the thought that Jesus must honor his mother and therefore, still in heaven listen to her.

> Finally, through Mary, the Holy Spirit begins to bring men, the objects of God's merciful love, into communion with Christ. (725)
>
> This motherhood of Mary in the order of grace continues uninterruptedly from the consent which she loyally gave at the Annunciation and which she sustained without wavering beneath the cross, until the eternal fulfilment of all the elect. Taken up to heaven she did not lay aside this saving office but by her manifold intercession continues to bring us the gifts of eternal salvation .... Therefore the Blessed Virgin is invoked in the Church under the titles of Advocate, Helper, Benefactress, and Mediatrix. (969)
>
> Mary's function as mother of men in no way obscures or diminishes this unique mediation of Christ, but rather

> shows its power. ... just as the priesthood of Christ is shared in various ways both by his ministers and the faithful, and as the one goodness of God is radiated in different ways among his creatures, so also the unique mediation of the Redeemer does not exclude but rather gives rise to a manifold cooperation which is but a sharing in this one source . (970)
>
> Ask the Mother of God to intercede for us. (1014)

Eternal State

The RCC believes that at the point of death every individual will be held accountable for his or her acceptance or denial of divine grace (1021). In which case the person will either enter:

1. Immediately into hell,

2. Immediately into heaven, or

3. Eventually into heaven after a time spent in purgatory

The RCC teaches that there will be a final judgment and accounting for the life on earth. Below are some paragraphs to support the RCC view of this judgment.

> Death puts an end to human life as the time open to either accepting or rejecting the divine grace manifested in Christ. The New Testament speaks of judgment primarily in its aspect of the final encounter with Christ in his second coming, but also repeatedly affirms that each will be rewarded immediately after death in accordance with his works and faith. (1021)
>
> Each man receives his eternal retribution in his immortal soul at the very moment of his death, in a particular judgment that refers his life to Christ: either entrance into the blessedness of heaven-through a purification or immediately,—or immediate and everlasting damnation. At the evening of life, we shall be judged on our love. (1022)

> The message of the Last Judgment calls men to conversion while God is still giving them the acceptable time, . . . the day of salvation (1041)

> Every man receives his eternal recompense in his immortal soul from the moment of his death in a particular judgment by Christ, the judge of the living and the dead. (1051)

> [T]he day of resurrection, death will be definitively conquered, when these souls will be reunited with their bodies. (1052)

> The holy Roman Church firmly believes and confesses that on the Day of Judgment all men will appear in their own bodies before Christ's tribunal to render an account of their own deeds. (1059)

> At the end of time, the Kingdom of God will come in its fullness. Then the just will reign with Christ for ever, glorified in body and soul, and the material universe itself will be transformed. God will then be "all in all" (1 Cor 15:28), in eternal life. (1060)

Heaven

Heaven is the final resting place for those accepting of divine grace (1023). The current activity in heaven involves Mary and the saints interceding for people on earth (956, 962).

Heaven is a place where Jesus and Mary are. It is also a place where the saints are giving of the grace that they have merited to those still on earth (2027). The problem is that if Mary has earned all merit, why has she not given it out to every person on earth? This logic shows the flaw in RCC theology of Mary's sinlessness, the saint's intercession and the grace merited from the dead given to the living.

Below are more paragraphs to support the RCC view of heaven.

> The intercession of the saints. "Being more closely united to Christ, those who dwell in heaven fix the whole Church more firmly in holiness.... They do not cease to intercede

with the Father for us, as they proffer the merits which they acquired on earth through the one mediator between God and men, Christ Jesus. (956)

We believe in the communion of all the faithful of Christ, those who are pilgrims on earth, the dead who are being purified, and the blessed in heaven, all together forming one Church; and we believe that in this communion, the merciful love of God and his saints is always [attentive] to our prayers. (962)

Those who die in God's grace and friendship and are perfectly purified live for ever with Christ. They are like God for ever, for they see him as he is, face to face: By virtue of our apostolic authority, we define the following: According to the general disposition of God, the souls of all the saints . . . and other faithful who died after receiving Christ's holy Baptism (provided they were not in need of purification when they died, . . . or, if they then did need or will need some purification, when they have been purified after death, . . .). (1023)

This perfect life with the Most Holy Trinity—this communion of life and love with the Trinity, with the Virgin Mary, the angels and all the blessed—is called "heaven." Heaven is the ultimate end and fulfillment of the deepest human longings, the state of supreme, definitive happiness. (1024)

To live in heaven is to be with Christ. The elect live in Christ, but they retain, or rather find, their true identity, their own name. For life is to be with Christ; where Christ is, there is life, there is the kingdom. (1025)

In this new universe, the heavenly Jerusalem, God will have his dwelling among men. He will wipe away every tear from their eyes, and death shall be no more, neither shall there be mourning nor crying nor pain any more, for the former things have passed away. (1044)

The visible universe, then, is itself destined to be transformed, so that the world itself, restored to its original

> state, facing no further obstacles, should be at the service of the just, sharing their glorification in the risen Jesus Christ. (1047)
>
> We believe that the multitude of those gathered around Jesus and Mary in Paradise forms the Church of heaven, where in eternal blessedness they see God as he is and where they are also, to various degrees, associated with the holy angels in the divine governance exercised by Christ in glory, by interceding for us and helping our weakness by their fraternal concern. (1053)

Hell

Hell is the final un-resting place for those rejecting divine grace (1022). Hell is a literal place that contains conscience people for all eternity for the purpose of punishment (1033).

There is question by what is meant that Christ preached the gospel to the souls in hell. The RCC teaches that it was necessary to bring the gospel message to complete fulfillment (634). It seems that the dead had a second chance to believe (635). However, the dead referred to could be those still in purgatory. However, then they would not need to hear the gospel. They would need to just wait and do their time.

Below are some more paragraphs to support the RCC view of hell.

> The gospel was preached even to the dead. The descent into hell brings the Gospel message of salvation to complete fulfillment. (634)
>
> Christ went down into the depths of death so that the dead will hear the voice of the Son of God, and those who hear will live. (635)
>
> We cannot be united with God unless we freely choose to love him. But we cannot love God if we sin gravely against him, against our neighbor or against ourselves: He who does not love remains in death. ... To die in mortal sin without repenting and accepting God's merciful love means

remaining separated from him for ever by our own free choice. This state of definitive self- exclusion from communion with God and the blessed is called hell. (1033)

The teaching of the Church affirms the existence of hell and its eternity. Immediately after death the souls of those who die in a state of mortal sin descend into hell, where they suffer the punishments of hell, eternal fire. The chief punishment of hell is eternal separation from God, in whom alone man can possess the life and happiness for which he was created and for which he longs. (1035)

God predestines no one to go to hell; for this, a willful turning away from God (a mortal sin) is necessary, and persistence in it until the end. (1037)

Hell's principal punishment consists of eternal separation from God in whom alone man can have the life and happiness for which he was created and for which he longs. (1057)

Purgatory

Purgatory is a place of temporal punishment for sins committed on earth that still need payment (1022). Those still on earth can reduce the time that loved ones spend in purgatory by indulgences offered up on behalf of the dead (958, 1023).

The RCC's doctrine of purgatory is an affront to the finished work of Christ on the cross. This doctrine is based on the belief that the forgiveness of sins is not based on the work of Christ but the payment of the sinner in penance on earth or punishment after death. Thus, the RCC teaches, by implication, salvation by works not by faith.

Another problem with this doctrine is that sin has an eternal consequence not a temporal one. Therefore, the time required to pay for even one "small" sin is all eternity. Thus, purgatory would need to be renamed "hell".

So the living earn merits for the dead in purgatory, like the dead in heaven do for the living on earth (2027). Why not have the living earn merits for the living and let the dead take care of the dead? This logic shows the flaw in earning merit or grace for another, dead or alive. Our salvation is not based on our own works, so how could another's work merit grace, unless that other was the sinless Christ.

Below are some more paragraphs to support the RCC view of purgatory.

> Communion with the dead. In full consciousness of this communion of the whole Mystical Body of Jesus Christ, the Church in its pilgrim members, from the very earliest days of the Christian religion, has honored with great respect the memory of the dead; and 'because it is a holy and a wholesome thought to pray for the dead that they may be loosed from their sins' she offers her suffrages for them. Our prayer for them is capable not only of helping them, but also of making their intercession for us effective. (958)
>
> Those who die in God's grace and friendship and are perfectly purified live for ever with Christ. They are like God for ever, for they see him as he is, face to face: By virtue of our apostolic authority, we define the following: According to the general disposition of God, the souls of all the saints . . . and other faithful who died after receiving Christ's holy Baptism (provided they were not in need of purification when they died, . . . or, if they then did need or will need some purification, when they have been purified after death, . . .). (1023)
>
> All who die in God's grace and friendship, but still imperfectly purified, are indeed assured of their eternal salvation; but after death they undergo purification, so as to achieve the holiness necessary to enter the joy of heaven. (1030)
>
> The Church gives the name Purgatory to this final purification of the elect, which is entirely different from the punishment of the damned. The Church formulated her doctrine of faith on Purgatory especially at the Councils of Florence and Trent. The tradition of the Church, by reference to certain texts of Scripture, speaks of a

cleansing fire: As for certain lesser faults, we must believe that, before the Final Judgment, there is a purifying fire. He who is truth says that whoever utters blasphemy against the Holy Spirit will be pardoned neither in this age nor in the age to come. From this sentence we understand that certain offenses can be forgiven in this age, but certain others in the age to come. (1031)

This teaching is also based on the practice of prayer for the dead, already mentioned in Sacred Scripture: Therefore [Judas Maccabeus] made atonement for the dead, that they might be delivered from their sin. From the beginning the Church has honored the memory of the dead and offered prayers in suffrage for them, above all the Eucharistic sacrifice, so that, thus purified, they may attain the beatific vision of God. The Church also commends almsgiving, indulgences, and works of penance undertaken on behalf of the dead: Let us help and commemorate them. If Job's sons were purified by their father's sacrifice, why would we doubt that our offerings for the dead bring them some consolation? Let us not hesitate to help those who have died and to offer our prayers for them. (1032)

Those who die in God's grace and friendship imperfectly purified, although they are assured of their eternal salvation, undergo a purification after death, so as to achieve the holiness necessary to enter the joy of God. (1054)

virtue of the "communion of saints," the Church commends the dead to God's mercy and offers her prayers, especially the holy sacrifice of the Eucharist, on their behalf. (1055)

In the communion of saints, a perennial link of charity exists between the faithful who have already reached their heavenly home, those who are expiating their sins in purgatory and those who are still pilgrims on earth. between them there is, too, an abundant exchange of all good things. In this wonderful exchange, the holiness of one profits others, well beyond the harm that the sin of one could cause others. Thus recourse to the communion of saints lets the contrite sinner be more promptly and efficaciously purified of the punishments for sin. (1475)

Chapter 3

Islam

Islam is the name given to the religion founded by Muhammad of Arabia in the early seventh century. The word ISLAM is derived from the verb SLM to resign, surrender or submit oneself. iSLaM means the act of submission and of resignation of oneself. One who professes Islam is a muSLiM, one who has submitted. The word Muslim finds it root the same as the word for peace, salaam.

Islam is the youngest of the world's major religions originated in the seventh century with the life and mission of Muhammad. It was not a totally new religion. Its conceptual roots are in Judaism and Christianity. Muslims see their religion as a continuation and rectification of the Judeo-Christian tradition.

Born in Mecca 570 A.D, Muhammad was an illiterate, orphan slave of a wealthy widow, whom he eventually married. By his marriage, he became a person of importance and was able to find time for uninterrupted meditation on religious matters. He was concerned about the idolatry and polytheism of his countrymen. Forced out of Mecca because of his teachings, he and his followers moved to Medina, where he developed his teaching more fully. Muhammad used his teachings of Islam to unite many Arab tribes in warfare against enemies. Islam won much of the Middle East by force.

Muhammad Background[7]

Muhammad was born in the wealthy merchant town of Mecca, which was a very important trading centre for western Arabia. It stood on the main caravan routes joining the land-borne trade of the Arabian Peninsula with the maritime trade of the Red Sea, thus linking India to the West and Africa to Persia.

Mecca was also famous for its shrine, the Kaba. This cube-like building was the center of a cult of sacred stones including the 'Black Stone', said to have come from heaven, which is built into the eastern corner of the Kaba. The Kaba was a centre of annual pilgrimage for tribes throughout Arabia.

Muslim historians refer to the religious situation in Arabia before the advent of Islam as 'the times of ignorance'. The Arabs were largely idolatrous and polytheistic. According to some sources, as many as 360 deities were worshipped at the Kaba.

Muhammad's Early Life

The earliest accounts of Muhammad's life were written at least 150 years after his death. All are Muslim sources and there is no external supporting evidence.

Muhammad was born in A.D. 570, a few months after the death of his father Abdullah. His family belonged to the Quraysh tribe, at the time the custodians of the Kaba. His mother, Aminah, died when he was six. His paternal uncle, Abu Talib, brought him up. Tradition says that on a caravan convoy with his uncle, he met a Nestorian monk who, according to some Muslim commentators, perceived that Muhammad was a prophet. When Muhammad grew up to manhood, he became an esteemed member of the merchant's guild at Mecca. He joined the caravan trading routes, making contacts with Jews and Christians, with whom he discussed religion in connection with the Old and New Testaments.

Many non-Muslims have thought Muhammad to be a deliberate impostor, but perhaps he was at first a genuine seeker after divine truth, who was dissatisfied with the Christian witness of his time as well as the idolatrous state of his own people in Arabia. The Christian witnesses that Muhammad had met were those forced out of the Roman Empire due to their heresies. Muhammad had not contacted genuine Christianity, but instead heresies that disputed over issues of the Deity of Christ and the Trinity.

Khadijah, a wealthy widow, employed Muhammad to manage her caravan trade. Muhammad was a slave to Khadijah. Although she was fifteen years older then he, Muhammad married Khadijah when he was twenty-five. The marriage produced seven children (three sons and four daughters), all of whom died young, except a daughter, Fatimah, who became the wife of Ali-ibn-Abu Talib and mother of Hassan and Hussain. Khadijah died twenty-five years later. After her death Muhammad married a further twelve wives, thereby sanctioning polygamy.

Muhammad's Life and Call

By his marriage Muhammad became a person of importance and was able to find time for uninterrupted meditation on religious matters. At about the age of forty, he became very concerned about the irreligion of his fellow countrymen and began to retire frequently miles from Mecca. During these periods of meditation, he seemed at times to be in a kind of trance; while in this condition he claimed he heard the voice of Allah or the Archangel Gabriel, who gave him messages to preach to mankind. Since, he was illiterate his entire life he did not write down these messages, but instead taught them to his converts who memorized that and wrote them down after his death, in what became the Qur'an.

The First Converts

Muhammad's first followers were chiefly members of his own family—his wife Khadijah, his nephew Ali-ibn-Abu Talib and Zaid, an adopted son who had formerly been his slave, a gift to Muhammad from Khadijah. The first adult outside the family to make profession of Islam was Abu Bakr, a wealthy merchant, who was a significant early convert.

Muhammad's Flight to Medina and the Development of His Teaching

Most of the inhabitants of Mecca rejected Muhammad's teaching about the true Allah and his warning of the coming judgement. They accused him of being a soothsayer or demon-possessed. Growing hostility on the part of the rulers and people of the city lod to violent persecution of the Muslims. Nevertheless there was a gradual increase in his followers, who numbered approximately fifty during the period 610-613.

As the opposition intensified, Muhammad decided to leave Mecca and seek asylum elsewhere. He first sent a number of his followers to the Christian kingdom of Abyssinia, but he himself settled at Yathrib, a city 250 miles north of Mecca, which is now called Medina [city, i.e. the Prophet's own city]. The people of Media were favourably disposed towards Muhammad and the new teaching. A party of its inhabitants, who had met him, accepted his claims and prepared their fellow townsmen for his advent had invited him there. The citizens, wearied by long internal strife, were ready to welcome a strong leader who might unite them. Jews and Christians were at this time sympathetic to Muhammad's teaching with its emphasis on the unity of God and accompanying condemnation of idolatry.

The move from Mecca to Medina took place in the year 622. This flight to hijrah was the turning point in Muhammad's career and chosen to mark the beginning of the Muslim era and calendar. In 624, Muhammad's forces gained a decisive victory at the Battle of Badr. The decision to give shares in the booty to those who fought with him swung the military balance in his favour. Henceforth, war on religious grounds was but a religious duty for Muslims when Islam is under threat.

At first, Muhammad recognized the validity of the Jewish and Christian faiths, being content to preach as the prophet to his own people. Muslims faced Jerusalem when praying and he adopted several Jewish practices. However, friction developed when the Jewish tribes failed to recognize him as a true prophet or to practice the customs of Islam. Troubled by this, Muhammad began to assert the absolute character of the revelation that had been given to him and claimed it was a renewal of the religion that Abraham had professed. In this way, he gave up any attempt to reconcile Islam with Judaism. The Muslim community was now commanded to face the Kaba at Mecca when praying, not Jerusalem.

During Muhammad's time in Medina, his doctrine took shape. He changed the direction of prayer and other areas of his early teaching. At Medina, he began to teach that the Qur'an was the final and superior revelation. The daily times of prayer with preliminary washings now became obligatory. He appointed

Friday the day for corporate worship at the mosque. The annual month of fasting was established.

In Medina, Muhammad became a statesman, legislator and judge. As his people and influence increased so did large-scale warfare. In the eight years following the hijrah, Muslim armies succeeded in conquering the whole of Arabia and stamping on it the religion of Islam. Muhammad was the first person to unify the Arabs as one people.

Death of Muhammad and the Expansion of Islam

Muhammad died in 632 at the age of sixty-two and Caliph by Abu Bakr, one of his earliest followers, succeeded him. Under Abu Baker, Islam was consolidated as a stable power and Syria fell to its advancing armies.

Abu Bakr was succeeded in 634 by Caliph Umar, who was in turn succeeded by Caliph Uthman in 644. During this time Iraq, Persian and Egypt fell in quick succession and by 656, the boundaries of Islam had reached Afghanistan in the east, Libya in the west and the Caucasus mountains in the north. The conquest of the remainder of North Africa and advance through Spain into France was only halted in 732 at one of history's crucial battles, fought on a site between Tours and Poitiers.

Reasons for such a rapid expansion are not hard to find. The collapse of the Byzantine Empire had created a political vacuum. The dynamic leadership of Muhammad was able to exploit the Arab peoples who, for so long had been divided along tribal lines they were now united under new leadership and more able to make a positive thrust, first into the lands surrounding the Arabian Peninsula and then further advancing into North Africa and Europe.

With the notable exception of the Copts in Egypt, the Christian Church in North Africa was defeated and overthrown. The Church which had known the leadership of such men as Augustine, Athanasius, Cyprian and Tertullian found itself quite unable to resist the advancing armies of Islam. The ruins of ancient church buildings are the sole remains of a once vigorous Church.

Sunni and Shiah split

Islam has two main divisions: Sunni and Shiah. Sunni Muslims form the majority (about 90 percent). Shiah Muslims are a majority only in Iran. The split originated in a dispute over leadership succession little more than twenty years after Muhammad's death. Muhammad's successors were known as caliphs and the first three were Abu Baker in 632, Umar in 634 and Uthman in 644. the fourth caliph, who succeeded in 656, was Ali, the husband of Muhammad's daughter Fatima. He was not universally accepted as the rightful successor and Muslims began to fight each other over the issue. Ali was eventually murdered in 661 and his two sons, Hassan and Hussain, continued the struggle. Hassan was poisoned in about 670 and Hussaim died at the Battle of Karbala in 680. Ali's followers, Shiah Ali [the party of Ali], became the Shiah Muslims.

Authority

Jewish and Christian Scriptures

Muslims believe that Allah has revealed his commands to men through his prophets and through 104 sacred books. Of these books, only four now remain that where written by the "prophets".

Moses—the Taurah, the Pentateuch

David—the Zabur, the Psalms

Jesus—the Injil, the Gospels or the N.T. in general

Muhammad—the Qur'an

Although Islam claims credit to David for the Psalms and Jesus for the Gospels or the New Testament, David did not write all of the Psalms and Jesus did not write any part of the New Testament, whereas the others writers did write or dictate their works. Muslims claim that the Old and New Testaments have been distorted, however, somehow the Qur'an could not have been distorted, nor does it state what is corrupted in them. If only 4 of 104 books remain of the sacred writings of God then He does not have a good track record of ensuring that His Word will be preserved. Therefore, how can we trust the Qur'an?

Muhammad did not claim to bring a completely new revelation, or to establish a new religion. His concern was to bring his people back to the original religion professed and preached by all the prophets from Adam onwards.

> Say ye: 'We believe in Allah, and the revelation given to us, and to Abraham, Isma'il, Isaac, Jacob, and the Tribes, and that given to Moses and Jesus, and that given to (all) Prophets from their Lord: we make no difference between one and another of them: and we bow to Allah (in Islam).' (Q 2:136)

> We have sent thee inspiration, as We sent it to Noah and the Messengers after him: we sent inspiration to Abraham, Isma'il, Isaac, Jacob and the Tribes, to Jesus, Job, Jonah, Aaron, and Solomon, and to David We gave the Psalms. (Q 4:163)

> If thou wert in doubt as to what We have revealed unto thee, then ask those who have been reading the Book from before thee: the Truth hath indeed come to thee from thy Lord: so be in no wise of those in doubt. (Q 10:94)

There are over 120 references in the Qur'an to the Scriptures of the Jews and Christians, testifying to their being genuine revelations from Allah. The Jews and Christians are referred to as 'the people of the Book'.

> It was We who revealed the law (to Moses): therein was guidance and light. By its standard have been judged the Jews, by the prophets who bowed (as in Islam) to Allah's will, by the rabbis and the doctors of law: for to them was entrusted the protection of Allah's book, and they were witnesses thereto: therefore fear not men, but fear me, and sell not my signs for a miserable price. If any do fail to judge by (the light of) what Allah hath revealed, they are (no better than) Unbelievers. ... And in their footsteps We sent Jesus the son of Mary, confirming the Law that had come before him: We sent him the Gospel: therein was

> guidance and light, and confirmation of the Law that had come before him: a guidance and an admonition to those who fear Allah. ... To thee We sent the Scripture in truth, confirming the scripture that came before it, and guarding it in safety: so judge between them by what Allah hath revealed, and follow not their vain desires, diverging from the Truth that hath come to thee. To each among you have we prescribed a law and an open way. If Allah had so willed, He would have made you a single people, but (His plan is) to test you in what He hath given you: so strive as in a race in all virtues. The goal of you all is to Allah. it is He that will show you the truth of the matters in which ye dispute; (Q 5:44, 46, 48)

Muslims claim that Jews and Christians changed and distorted their own Scriptures, so Allah sent the Qur'an as the final revelation to humanity. The previous scriptures (everything prior to the Qur'an) were meant for a limited period. Their use ended with the revelation of the Qur'an, which abrogated them and exposed their distortions and changes. That is why they were not protected from corruption. They underwent distortion, addition, and omission.

People of the Book! Our Messenger has come to you, making clear to you many things you have been concealing of the Book and forgiving you of much. A light has come to you from Allah and a glorious Book, with which He will guide whoever follows His pleasure in the way of peace, and brings them forth from darkness into the light by His will. (Q 5:15-16)

> And there is a group among them who twist their tongues with the Book, that you may think it is a part of the Book but it is not part of the Book. And they say 'It is from Allah,' yet it is not from Allah, and they tell a lie against Allah and they know it. It is not for any human being to whom Allah has given the Book, the Wisdom and the Prophet hood to say to men 'Worship me instead of Allah". (Q 3:79)

> So woe to those who write the Book with their hands, and then say: 'This is from Allah,' that they may sell it for a little price. So woe to them for what their hands have written, and woe to them for their earnings. (Q 2:79)

> Say, who sent down the Book that Moses brought as a light and a guidance to people? You put it into sheets of paper showing some of them and concealing much. (Q 6:91)

The Qur'an was to be permanent and not to be questioned as the other Scriptures. "Do they not consider the Qur'an (with care)? Had it been from other than Allah, they would surely have found therein much discrepancy." (Q 4:82)

Qur'an

The word 'Qur'an' is derived from the Arabic word q*ara* meaning 'to read' or 'to recite'.

The Qur'an is about the same length as the New Testament and is divided into 114 surahs (chapters). The surahs are not arranged in chronological order but roughly in order of length. With the exception of surah 1, which is a prayer addressed to Allah, it is Allah himself and not the prophet who is the speaker.

The Qur'an, the sacred book of Islam, is believed to have been revealed to Muhammad by the angel Gabriel 'piecemeal' as occasion required during the last twenty-three years of his life. Muslims take a fundamentalist attitude to God's Word and the Qur'an holds a place of exalted reverence in their hearts. The Qur'an is said to have existed eternally in heaven engraved on a stone tablet. The language of this archetype is Arabic. Therefore, that language is inherently of a stature unattainable by any other. Speakers of Arabic have a special prestige in the eyes of the Muslim world.

Muhammad claimed the Qur'an was revealed to him when he was under the control of the spirits. He testified that he himself was not always certain whether the visions were divine or demonic. However, his wife urged him to submit to the revelations, because she was convinced they were from Gabriel. Therefore, for twenty-two years, from A.D. 610 until his death in A.D. 632, he received revelations from the spirit that controlled him. These were collected, memorized and passed down orally at first. Soon his followers, from memory, compiled them, forming the Qur'an.

Muhammad passed on the revelations orally to his companions, some of whom wrote them down while others memorized them. Muslim orthodoxy holds that the angel Gabriel helped Muhammad to collate the revelations periodically so that at his death there was an exact transcript of what was written on the heavenly tablet.

Modern scholarship, however, has shown that there was no complete set of collated and arranged revelations at Muhammad's death. Some time after his death the revelations were assembled by Muslim leaders from records written on leaves, stones, camel's shoulder-blades, etc. and from the memories of those who had stored the revelations in their minds. The resulting collections of revelation made in different places varied somewhat from each other. Caliph Uthman decided to bring order to the situation and had scholars create an official standard text between 650 and 656, which he circulated widely while ordering all other versions to be destroyed.

Muhammad built his whole system of religion on these demonic revelations, adapting and merging various forms and features from the idol worship that had always existed in Mecca. His stress on monotheism was the novelty that ultimately unified Islam.

Sunnah

The Sunnah are the writings of what the prophet Muhammad said, did or approved of, comprised of hadeeths, which are reliably transmitted reports by the prophet Muhammad's companions.

Shrariah—Islamic Law

Where the Qur'an and traditions are silent on a particular subject, rules are derived by consensus of the religious leaders [ijma] and by analogous reasoning [qiyas]. The combination of Qur'an, hadith, ijma and qiyas have been used by Islamic scholars to create the immensely detailed body of rules and regulations known as the Shariah, that is, Islamic law.

Four orthodox schools are recognized in Sunni Islam:

Hanafi: founded by Imam abu Hanifa (died 767)

Maliki: founded by Imam Malik ibn Anas (died 795)

Shafii: founded by Imam Muhammad bin Idris ash Shafi'I (died 820)

Hanbali: founded by Imam Ahmad ibn Hanbal (died 855)

God

Paganism is offensive to a Muslim. Islam believes in strict monotheism. Islam does not accept any God that has multiple persons as a Godhead. They would believe that to be polytheism. Islam denies the Trinity because it misunderstands the definition to be referring to the three gods as consisting of Father (Allah), Mother (Mary) and Son (Jesus).

> O People of the Book! Commit no excesses in your religion: Nor say of Allah anything but the truth. Christ Jesus the son of Mary was (no more than) an apostle of Allah, and His Word, which He bestowed on Mary, and a spirit proceeding from Him: so believe in Allah and His apostles. Say not "Trinity": desist: it will be better for you: for Allah is one Allah. Glory be to Him: (far exalted is He) above having a son. To Him belong all things in the heavens and on earth. And enough is Allah as a Disposer of affairs. (Q 4:171)

> And behold! Allah will say: "O Jesus the son of Mary! Didst thou say unto men, worship me and my mother as gods in derogation of Allah.?" He will say: "Glory to Thee! never could I say what I had no right (to say). Had I said such a thing, thou wouldst indeed have known it. Thou knowest what is in my heart, though I know not what is in Thine. For Thou knowest in full all that is hidden. (Q 5:116)

> Say: He is Allah, the One and Only; Allah, the Eternal, Absolute; He begetteth not, nor is He begotten; And there is none like unto Him. (Q 112)

> They do blaspheme who say: Allah is one of three in a Trinity: for there is no god except One Allah. If they desist not from their word (of blasphemy), verily a grievous penalty will befall the blasphemers among them. Why turn

> they not to Allah, and seek His forgiveness? For Allah is Oft- forgiving, Most Merciful. Christ the son of Mary was no more than an apostle; many were the apostles that passed away before him. His mother was a woman of truth. They had both to eat their (daily) food. See how Allah doth make His signs clear to them; yet see in what ways they are deluded away from the truth! (Q 5:73-75)

The belief in a Trinity is the only unforgivable sin in Islam.

> Allah forgiveth not that partners should be set up with Him; but He forgiveth anything else, to whom He pleaseth; to set up partners with Allah is to devise a sin most heinous indeed. (Q 4:48)

Jesus Christ

Islam often refers to Jesus as "the son of Mary". This phrase displays that he is merely human not Divine. Jesus is a messenger of Allah, along with Abraham, Moses and Noah.

> And remember We took from the prophets their covenant: As (We did) from thee: from Noah, Abraham, Moses, and Jesus the son of Mary: We took from them a solemn covenant: (Q 33:7)

> The same religion has He established for you as that which He enjoined on Noah—the which We have sent by inspiration to thee—and that which We enjoined on Abraham, Moses, and Jesus: Namely, that ye should remain steadfast in religion, and make no divisions therein: to those who worship other things than Allah, hard is the (way) to which thou callest them. Allah chooses to Himself those whom He pleases, and guides to Himself those who turn (to Him). (Q 42:13)

Instead of Jesus interceding with the Father on behalf of Christians, Muslims believe that Muhammad intercedes for them to Allah. Muhammad will plead with Allah, after His permission and on behalf of humanity, to judge among His servants when they suffer from worries and troubles that they cannot bear. They will go to Adam, then to Noah, then to Abraham, then to Moses, then to Jesus, and finally to Muhammad. Muslims believe in the intercession that concerns some believers who were to be taken out from the fire. This mediation is granted to Muhammad and to others among the prophets, the believers, and the angels. Allah will save from hell some of the believers without the intercession of any one, but by His grace and mercy.

Born of a Virgin

Islam believes that Jesus was born of a virgin named Mary. Islam accepts a supernatural conception of Jesus but a normal conception and birth for Muhammad, the greatest and final prophet.

> Behold! the angels said: "O Mary! Allah giveth thee glad tidings of a Word from Him: his name will be Christ Jesus, the son of Mary, held in honour in this world and the Hereafter and of (the company of) those nearest to Allah. "He shall speak to the people in childhood and in maturity. And he shall be (of the company) of the righteous." She said: "O my Lord! How shall I have a son when no man hath touched me?" He said: "Even so: Allah createth what He willeth: When He hath decreed a plan, He but saith to it, 'Be,' and it is! (Q 3:45-47)

> Relate in the Book (the story of) Mary, when she withdrew from her family to a place in the East. She placed a screen (to screen herself) from them; then We sent her our angel, and he appeared before her as a man in all respects. She said: "I seek refuge from thee to ((Allah)) Most Gracious: (come not near) if thou dost fear Allah." He said: "Nay, I am only a messenger from thy Lord, (to announce) to thee the gift of a holy son. She said: "How shall I have a son, seeing that no man has touched me, and I am not unchaste?" He said: "So (it will be): Thy Lord saith, 'that is easy for Me: and (We wish) to appoint him as a Sign unto men and a Mercy from Us':It is a matter (so) decreed." So she conceived him, and she retired with him to a remote place. (Q 19:16-22)

> And Mary the daughter of 'Imran, who guarded her chastity; and We breathed into (her body) of Our spirit; and she testified to the truth of the words of her Lord and of His Revelations, and was one of the devout (servants). (Q 66:12)

Deity of Christ

Islam clearly denies the Deity of Christ.

> [Jesus] was no more than a servant: We granted Our favour to him, and We made him an example to the Children of Israel. (Q 43:59)

> They do blaspheme who say: "(Allah) is Christ the son of Mary." But said Christ: "O Children of Israel! worship Allah, my Lord and your Lord." Whoever joins other gods with Allah,- Allah will forbid him the garden, and the Fire will be his abode. There will for the wrong-doers be no one to help. (Q 5:72)

> Say: He is Allah, the One and Only; Allah, the Eternal, Absolute; He begetteth not, nor is He begotten; And there is none like unto Him. (Q 112)

> The similitude of Jesus before Allah is as that of Adam; He created him from dust, then said to him: "Be". And he was. (Q 3:59)

> Such (was) Jesus the son of Mary: (it is) a statement of truth, about which they (vainly) dispute. It is not befitting to (the majesty of) Allah that He should beget a son. Glory be to Him! when He determines a matter, He only says to it, "Be", and it is. (Q 19:34-35)

> O People of the Book! Commit no excesses in your religion: Nor say of Allah anything but the truth. Christ Jesus the son of Mary was (no more than) an apostle of Allah, and His Word, which He bestowed on Mary, and a spirit proceeding from Him: so believe in Allah and His apostles. Say not "Trinity" : desist: it will be better for you: for Allah is one Allah. Glory be to Him: (far exalted is He)

> above having a son. To Him belong all things in the heavens and on earth. And enough is Allah as a Disposer of affairs. (Q 4:171)

> And behold! Allah will say: "O Jesus the son of Mary! Didst thou say unto men, worship me and my mother as gods in derogation of Allah.?" He will say: "Glory to Thee! never could I say what I had no right (to say). Had I said such a thing, thou wouldst indeed have known it. Thou knowest what is in my heart, though I know not what is in Thine. For Thou knowest in full all that is hidden. (Q 5:116)

> To Him is due the primal origin of the heavens and the earth: How can He have a son when He hath no consort? He created all things, and He hath full knowledge of all things. That is Allah, your Lord! there is no god but He, the Creator of all things: then worship ye Him: and He hath power to dispose of all affairs. No vision can grasp Him, but His grasp is over all vision: He is above all comprehension, yet is acquainted with all things. "Now have come to you, from your Lord, proofs (to open your eyes): if any will see, it will be for (the good of) his own soul; if any will be blind, it will be to his own (harm): I am not (here) to watch over your doings." Thus do we explain the signs by various (symbols): that they may say, "Thou hast taught (us) diligently," and that We may make the matter clear to those who know. Follow what thou art taught by inspiration from thy Lord: there is no god but He: and turn aside from those who join gods with Allah. (Q 6:101-106)

Crucifixion of Christ

Islam denies the crucifixion of Christ and believes that Allah took Jesus from the earth and allowed a look-alike to be crucified in His place.

> That they [the Jews] rejected Faith; that they uttered against Mary a grave false charge; That they said (in boast), "We killed Christ Jesus the son of Mary, the Messenger of Allah.;- but they killed him not, nor crucified him, but so it was made to appear to them, and those who

> differ therein are full of doubts, with no (certain) knowledge, but only conjecture to follow, for of a surety they killed him not:- Nay, Allah raised him up unto Himself; and Allah is Exalted in Power, Wise; (Q 4:156-158)

However, if Christ did not die and was born from a supernatural conception that would make Jesus a greater prophet them Muhammad, who was conceived of natural means and died a natural death. Therefore, there is a reference of Jesus in the cradle claiming that he would die and some Muslims would state that Jesus will return to earth and then die. This ensures not only that Jesus would have a natural death but also handles the New Testament reference to Jesus' return.

> So Peace on him the day he was born, the day that he dies, and the day that he will be raised up to life (again)! ... But she pointed to the babe. They said: "How can we talk to one who is a child in the cradle?" He said: "I am indeed a servant of Allah. He hath given me revelation and made me a prophet; ... "So peace is on me the day I was born, the day that I die, and the day that I shall be raised up to life (again)"! Such (was) Jesus the son of Mary: (it is) a statement of truth, about which they (vainly) dispute. (Q 19:15, 29-30, 33-34)

Sin

Islam does not espouse the doctrine of original sin. Islam teaches that the sinner alone, the individual person and not his ancestors or descendants, is responsible for his actions; there is no inherited sin on the soul to be purged as a condition of entry into the faith. Islam teaches that all good is from Allah and all evil is from man.

> Whatever good, (O man!) happens to thee, is from Allah. but whatever evil happens to thee, is from thy (own) soul. and We have sent thee as an apostle to (instruct) mankind. And enough is Allah for a witness. (Q 4:79)

Salvation

Salvation to a Muslim seems to be based on a desire to avoid hell and receive pleasures and happiness. Throughout the Qur'an, the principal motivation for accepting God and believing in His revelation appears to be fear: fear of the last judgment and fear of eternal damnation. There is not as strong view of salvation from sin and reconciling with God for the purpose of worshiping Him that He receives all the glory, honor and praise.

No Muslim can know for sure where he is going in the afterlife. Allah through an absolute, arbitrary kind of determinism decides everyone's destiny. Most Muslims cling to the hope that good works might weigh heavily on Allah's scales of justice. But killing and being killed in jihad is the only sure pathway to heaven.

Most Muslims attach supreme importance to their duties. They believe, on the authority of the Qur'an, that salvation is by 'works'. Hence, their concern, even anxiety and fear, is to fulfill their duties.

The representation of a pair of scales on the walls of Muslim buildings conveys the idea of justice based on works of righteousness.

> Then those whose balance (of good deeds) is heavy,—they will attain salvation: But those whose balance is light, will be those who have lost their souls, in Hell will they abide. (Q 23:102-103)
>
> But those who believe and do deeds of righteousness, We shall soon admit to Gardens, with rivers flowing beneath,—their eternal home: Therein shall they have companions pure and holy: We shall admit them to shades, cool and ever deepening. (Q 4:57)
>
> But give glad tidings to those who believe and work righteousness, that their portion is Gardens, beneath which rivers flow. (Q 2:25a)

Five Pillars

Islam has a highly developed code of religious observance, referred to as the five pillars of faith.

1. Confessing the Faith

Recite the Islamic creed/confession of faith in Arabic: "There is no [true] god but Allah, and Muhammad is the messenger (Prophet) of Allah". Believe and recite it in the presence of two witnesses and you have converted to Islam. The creed forms the structure of the Call to Prayer.

2. Prayer

Recite the ritual prayer five times daily. These are memorized, rote prayers always chanted in Arabic. Before reciting their prayers Muslims must perform ablutions (wash hands, mouth, nostrils, face, arms, ears, neck and feet). The prayers are recited five times daily at very precise times. Bending, kneeling and prostration at exactly the right times are required during the recitation.

3. Giving of Alms (Zakat)

Give the religious tax and offering for the needy, 2.5 percent on cash, gold and jewelry. Higher rates exist on crops, animals, etc.

4. Fasting

Fast during the month of Ramadan. During daylight hours, no food, drink, tobacco or sexual intercourse are allowed. At night the fast is lifted. At the end of the month there is a very special festival to celebrate completion of the fast. Children, pregnant women, sick people, some travellers and soldiers in combat are exempted from the fast.

5. Pilgrimage to Mecca

Make a pilgrimage to the city of Mecca in Saudi Arabia. A Muslim must go at least once to Mecca if he or she has the money and their health allows. They go to the original "house of God" (the Kaba) in Mecca. One person can go on behalf of another. Such a person will gain merit and will be rewarded on the Last Day (Judgement Day).

Forgiveness

There is very little in the Qur'an about forgiveness in comparison with other subjects, which are dealt with at length. From what is mentioned, it is clear that it is regarded as a quite arbitrary act of Allah which has little, if any, moral basis, and requires no act of redemption or reconciliation.

> For those who reject Allah, is a terrible Penalty: but for those who believe and work righteous deeds, is Forgiveness, and a magnificent Reward. (Q 35:7)

> Allah forgiveth not that partners should be set up with Him; but He forgiveth anything else, to whom He pleaseth; to set up partners with Allah is to devise a sin most heinous indeed. (Q 4:48)

The forgiveness received at salvation is not from all sins, but only from past sins. When someone converts to Islam, God forgives all of his previous sins and evil deeds.

> A man called Amr came to the Prophet Muhammad and said, "Give me your right hand so that I may give you my pledge of loyalty." The Prophet stretched out his right hand. Amr withdrew his hand. The Prophet said: "What has happened to you, O Amr?" He replied, "I intend to lay down a condition." The Prophet asked: "What condition do you intend to put forward?" Amr said, "That God forgive my sins." The Prophet said: "Didn't you know that converting to Islam erases all previous sins?" (Narrated in Saheeh Muslim, #121, and Mosnad Ahmad, #17357)

After converting to Islam, the person will be rewarded for his or her good and bad deeds according to the following saying of the Prophet Muhammad :

> Your Lord, Who is blessed and exalted, is most merciful. If someone intends to do a good deed but does not do it, a good deed will be recorded for him. And if he does do it, (a

> reward of) ten to seven hundred or many more times (the reward of the good deed), will be recorded for him. And if someone intends to do a bad deed but does not do it, a good deed will be recorded for him. And if he does do it, a bad deed will be recorded against him or God will wipe it out. (Narrated in Mosnad Ahmad, #2515, and Saheeh Muslim, #131)

Eternal State

Paradise (Heaven)

The name most frequently given to paradise, the abode of the blessed, is *Janna* [garden]. The description of paradise in the Qur'an shows that it is essentially a place of sensual delights in which there are beautiful women, couches covered with rich brocades, flowing cups and luscious fruits.

Heaven is for the righteous. However, it is a man-centered not God- centered place. Men that entering paradise will receive the desires of their hearts and that based on values here on earth, this side of death.

> Verily for the Righteous there will be a fulfillment of (the heart's) desires; Gardens enclosed, and grapevines; Companions of equal age; And a cup full (to the brim). No vanity shall they hear therein, nor Untruth:—Recompense from thy Lord, a gift, (amply) sufficient, (Q 78:31-36)

> (Other) faces that Day will be joyful, Pleased with their striving,—In a Garden on high, Where they shall hear no (word) of vanity: Therein will be a bubbling spring: Therein will be Thrones (of dignity), raised on high, Goblets placed (ready), And cushions set in rows, And rich carpets (all) spread out. (Q 88:8-16)

> Then (there will be) the Companions of the Right Hand;—What will be the Companions of the Right Hand? And the Companions of the Left Hand,—what will be the Companions of the Left Hand? And those Foremost (in Faith) will be Foremost (in the Hereafter). These will be

> those Nearest to Allah. In Gardens of Bliss: A number of people from those of old, And a few from those of later times. (They will be) on Thrones encrusted (with gold and precious stones), Reclining on them, facing each other. Round about them will (serve) youths of perpetual (freshness), with goblets, (shining) beakers, and cups (filled) out of clear-flowing fountains: No after-ache will they receive there from, nor will they suffer intoxication: And with fruits, any that they may select: And the flesh of fowls, any that they may desire. And (there will be) Companions with beautiful, big, and lustrous eyes,- Like unto Pearls well-guarded. A Reward for the deeds of their past (life). Not frivolity will they hear therein, nor any taint of ill,- Only the saying, "Peace! Peace". The Companions of the Right Hand,- what will be the Companions of the Right Hand? (They will be) among Lote-trees without thorns, Among Talh trees with flowers (or fruits) piled one above another,- In shade long-extended, By water flowing constantly, And fruit in abundance. Whose season is not limited, nor (supply) forbidden, And on Thrones (of Dignity), raised high. We have created (their Companions) of special creation. And made them virgin—pure (and undefiled),— Beloved (by nature), equal in age,- For the Companions of the Right Hand. (Q 56:8-38)

Hellfire (Hell)

Hell is a place of fiery torment for sinners.

> Truly Hell is as a place of ambush, For the transgressors a place of destination: They will dwell therein for ages. Nothing cool shall they taste therein, nor any drink, Save a boiling fluid and a fluid, dark, murky, intensely cold, A fitting recompense (for them). For that they used not to fear any account (for their deeds), But they (impudently) treated Our Signs as false. And all things have We preserved on record. "So taste ye (the fruits of your deeds); for no increase shall We grant you, except in Punishment." (Q 78:21-30)

> The Companions of the Left Hand,—what will be the Companions of the Left Hand? (They will be) in the midst

of a Fierce Blast of Fire and in Boiling Water, And in the shades of Black Smoke: Nothing (will there be) to refresh, nor to please: For that they were wont to be indulged, before that, in wealth (and luxury), And persisted obstinately in wickedness supreme! (Q 56:41-46)

As to those who reject Faith, and die rejecting,- never would be accepted from any such as much gold as the earth contains, though they should offer it for ransom. For such is (in store) a penalty grievous, and they will find no helpers. (Q 3:91)

And what will explain to thee what Hell-Fire is? Naught doth it permit to endure, and naught doth it leave alone!—Darkening and changing the colour of man! … And (ask) of the Sinners: "What led you into Hell Fire?" They will say: "We were not of those who prayed; Nor were we of those who fed the indigent; But we used to talk vanities with vain talkers; And we used to deny the Day of Judgment, Until there came to us (the Hour) that is certain." Then will no intercession of (any) intercessors profit them. (Q 74:27-29, 41-48)

(The sentence will be:) "Throw, throw into Hell every contumacious Rejecter of Allah!—"Who forbade what was good, transgressed all bounds, cast doubts and suspicions; "Who set up another god beside Allah. Throw him into a severe penalty." (Q 50:24-26)

Chapter 4

Church of Jesus Christ of Latter Day Saints

The Articles of Faith

1. We believe in God, the Eternal Father, and in His Son, Jesus Christ, and in the Holy Ghost.

2. We believe that men will be punished for their own sins, and not for Adam's transgression.

3. We believe that through the Atonement of Christ, all mankind may be saved, by obedience to the laws and ordinances of the Gospel.

4. We believe that the first principles and ordinances of the Gospel are: first, Faith in the Lord Jesus Christ; second, Repentance; third, Baptism by immersion for the remission of sins; fourth, Laying on of hands for the gift of the Holy Ghost.

5. We believe that a man must be called of God, by prophecy, and by the laying on of hands by those who are in authority, to preach the Gospel and administer in the ordinances thereof.

6. We believe in the same organization that existed in the Primitive Church, namely, apostles, prophets, pastors, teachers, evangelists, and so forth.

7. We believe in the gift of tongues, prophecy, revelation, visions, healing, interpretation of tongues, and so forth.

8. We believe the Bible to be the word of God as far as it is translated correctly; we also believe the Book of Mormon to be the word of God.

9. We believe all that God has revealed, all that He does now reveal, and we believe that He will yet reveal many great and important things pertaining to the Kingdom of God.

10. We believe in the literal gathering of Israel and in the restoration of the Ten Tribes; that Zion (the New Jerusalem) will be built upon this the American continent; that Christ will reign personally upon the earth; and, that the earth will be renewed and receive its paradisiacal glory.

11. We claim the privilege of worshiping Almighty God according to the dictates of our own conscience, and allow all men the same privilege, let them worship how, where, or what they may.

12. We believe in being subject to kings, presidents, rulers, and magistrates, in obeying, honoring, and sustaining the law.

13. We believe in being honest, true, chaste, benevolent, virtuous, and in doing good to all men; indeed, we may say that we follow the admonition of Paul—We believe all things, we hope all things, we have endured many things, and hope to be able to endure all things. If there is anything virtuous, lovely, or of good report or praiseworthy, we seek after these things.

Authority

Bible

The eighth article of faith states, "We believe the Bible to be the word of God as far as it is translated correctly; we also believe the Book of Mormon to be the word of God." The acceptable translations are the King James Version of the Bible and the Joseph Smith Translation (JST).

Book of Mormon

The following are the opening pages to the Book of Mormon. They provide a good understanding of the LDS view of the Book of Mormon, its creation and beliefs foundation to LDS doctrines.

INTRODUCTION

The Book of Mormon is a volume of holy scripture comparable to the Bible. It is a record of God's dealings with the ancient inhabitants of the Americas and contains, as does the Bible, the fullness of the everlasting gospel.

The book was written by many ancient prophets by the spirit of prophecy and revelation. Their words, written on gold plates, were quoted and abridged by a prophet-historian named Mormon. The record gives an account of two great civilizations. One came from Jerusalem in 600 B.C., and afterward separated into two nations, known as the Nephites and the Lamanites. The other came much earlier when the Lord confounded the tongues at the Tower of Babel. This group is known as the Jaredites. After thousands of years, all were destroyed except the Lamanites, and they are the principal ancestors of the American Indians.

The crowning event recorded in the Book of Mormon is the personal ministry of the Lord Jesus Christ among the Nephites soon after his resurrection. It puts forth the doctrines of the gospel, outlines the plan of salvation, and tells men what they must do to gain peace in this life and eternal salvation in the life to come.

After Mormon completed his writings, he delivered the account to his son Moroni, who added a few words of his own and hid up the plates in the hill Cumorah. On September 21, 1823, the same Moroni, then a glorified, resurrected being, appeared to the Prophet Joseph Smith and instructed him relative to the ancient record and its destined translation into the English language.

In due course the plates were delivered to Joseph Smith, who translated them by the gift and power of God. The record is now published in many languages as a new and additional witness that Jesus Christ is the Son of the living God and that all who will come unto him and obey the laws and ordinances of his gospel may be saved.

Concerning this record the Prophet Joseph Smith said: "I told the brethren that the Book of Mormon was the most correct of any book on earth, and the keystone of our religion, and a man would get nearer to God by abiding by its precepts, than by any other book."

In addition to Joseph Smith, the Lord provided for eleven others to see the gold plates for themselves and to be special witnesses of the truth and divinity of the Book of Mormon. Their written testimonies are included herewith as "The Testimony of Three Witnesses" and "The Testimony of Eight Witnesses."

We invite all men everywhere to read the Book of Mormon, to ponder in their hearts the message it contains, and then to ask God, the Eternal Father, in the name of Christ if the book is true. Those who pursue this course and ask in faith will gain a testimony of its truth and divinity by the power of the Holy Ghost. (See Moroni 10: 3-5.)

Those who gain this divine witness from the Holy Spirit will also come to know by the same power that Jesus Christ is the Savior of the world, that Joseph Smith is his revelator and prophet in these last days, and that The Church of Jesus Christ of Latter-day Saints is the Lord's kingdom once again established on the earth, preparatory to the second coming of the Messiah.

THE TESTIMONY OF THREE WITNESSES

Be it known unto all nations, kindreds, tongues, and people, unto whom this work shall come: That we, through the grace of God the Father, and our Lord Jesus Christ, have seen the plates which contain this record, which is a record of the people of Nephi, and also of the Lamanites, their brethren, and also of the people of Jared, who came from the tower of which hath been spoken. And we also know that they have been translated by the gift and power of God, for his voice hath declared it unto us; wherefore we know of a surety that the work is true. And we also testify that we have seen the engravings which are upon the plates; and they have been shown unto us by the power of God, and not of man. And we declare with words of soberness, that an angel of God came down from heaven, and he brought and laid before our eyes, that we beheld and saw the plates, and the engravings thereon; and we know that it is by the grace of God the Father, and our Lord Jesus Christ, that we beheld and bear record that these things are true. And it is marvelous in our eyes. Nevertheless, the voice of the Lord commanded us that we should bear record of it; wherefore, to be obedient unto the commandments of God, we bear testimony of these things. And we know that if we are faithful in Christ, we shall rid our garments of the blood of all men, and be found spotless before the judgment-seat of Christ, and shall dwell with him eternally in the heavens. And the honor be to the Father, and to the Son, and to the Holy Ghost, which is one God. Amen.

OLIVER COWDERY
DAVID WHITMER
MARTIN HARRIS

THE TESTIMONY OF EIGHT WITNESSES

Be it known unto all nations, kindreds, tongues, and people, unto whom this work shall come: That Joseph Smith, Jun., the translator of this work, has shown unto us the plates of which hath been spoken, which have the appearance of gold; and as many of the leaves as the said Smith has translated we did handle with our hands; and we also saw the engravings thereon, all of which has the appearance of ancient work, and of curious workmanship. And this we bear record with words of soberness, that the said Smith has shown unto us, for we have seen and hefted, and know of a surety that the said Smith has got the plates of which we have spoken. And we give our names unto the world, to witness unto the world that which we have seen. And we lie not, God bearing witness of it.

CHRISTIAN WHITMER
JACOB WHITMER
PETER WHITMER, JUN.
JOHN WHITMER
HIRAM PAGE
JOSEPH SMITH, SEN.
HYRUM SMITH
SAMUEL H. SMITH

TESTIMONY OF THE PROPHET JOSEPH SMITH

The Prophet Joseph Smith's own words about the coming forth of the Book of Mormon are:

"On the evening of the . . . twenty-first of September [1823] . . . I betook myself to prayer and supplication to Almighty God . . . .

"While I was thus in the act of calling upon God, I discovered a light appearing in my room, which continued to increase until the room was lighter than at noonday, when immediately a personage appeared at my bedside, standing in the air, for his feet did not touch the floor.

"He had on a loose robe of most exquisite whiteness. It was a whiteness beyond anything earthly I had ever seen; nor do I believe that any earthly thing could be made to appear so exceedingly white and brilliant. His hands were naked, and his arms also, a little above the wrists; so, also, were his feet naked, as were his legs, a little above the ankles. His head and neck were also bare. I could discover that he had no other clothing on but this robe, as it was open, so that I could see into his bosom.

"Not only was his robe exceedingly white, but his whole person was glorious beyond description, and his countenance truly like lightning. The room was exceedingly light, but not so very bright as immediately around his person. When I first looked upon him, I was afraid; but the fear soon left me.

"He called me by name, and said unto me that he was a messenger sent from the presence of God to me, and that his name was Moroni; that God had a work for me to do; and that my name should be had for good and evil among all nations, kindreds, and tongues, or that it should be both good and evil spoken of among all people.

"He said there was a book deposited, written upon gold plates, giving an account of the former inhabitants of this continent, and the source from whence they sprang. He also said that the fullness of the everlasting Gospel was contained in it, as delivered by the Savior to the ancient inhabitants;

"Also, that there were two stones in silver bows—and these stones, fastened to a breastplate, constituted what is called the Urim and Thummim—deposited with the plates; and the possession and use of these stones were what constituted Seers in ancient or former times; and that God had prepared them for the purpose of translating the book.

* * * * * * *

"Again, he told me, that when I got those plates of which he had spoken—for the time that they should be obtained was not yet fulfilled—I should not show them to any person; neither the breastplate with the Urim and Thummim; only to those to whom I should be commanded to show them; if I did I should be destroyed. While he was conversing with me about the plates, the vision was opened to my mind that I could see the place where the plates were deposited, and that so clearly and distinctly that I knew the place again when I visited it.

"After this communication, I saw the light in the room begin to gather immediately around the person of him who had been speaking to me, and it continued to do so, until the room was again left dark, except just around him, when instantly I saw, as it were, a conduit open right up into heaven, and he ascended until he entirely disappeared, and the room was left as it had been before this heavenly light had made its appearance.

"I lay musing on the singularity of the scene, and marveling greatly at what had been told to me by this extraordinary messenger; when, in the midst of my meditation, I suddenly discovered that my room was again beginning to get lighted, and in an instant, as it were, the same heavenly messenger was again by my bedside.

"He commenced, and again related the very same things which he had done at his first visit, without the least variation; which having done, he informed me of great judgments which were coming upon the earth, with great desolations by famine, sword, and pestilence; and that these grievous judgments would come on the earth in this generation. Having related these things, he again ascended as he had done before.

"By this time, so deep were the impressions made on my mind, that sleep had fled from my eyes, and I lay overwhelmed in astonishment at what I had both seen and heard. But what was my surprise when again I beheld the same messenger at my bedside, and heard him rehearse or repeat over again to me the same things as before; and added a caution to me, telling me that Satan would try to tempt me (in consequence of the indigent circumstances of my father's family), to get the plates for the purpose of getting rich. This he forbade me, saying that I must have no other object in view in getting the plates but to glorify God, and must not be influenced by any other motive than that of building His kingdom; otherwise I could not get them.

"After this third visit, he again ascended into heaven as before, and I was again left to ponder on the strangeness of what I had just experienced; when almost immediately after the heavenly messenger had ascended from me the third time, the cock crowed, and I found that day was approaching, so that our interviews must have occupied the whole of that night.

"I shortly after arose from my bed, and, as usual, went to the necessary labors of the day; but, in attempting to work as at other times, I found my strength so exhausted as to render me entirely unable. My father, who was laboring along with me, discovered something to be wrong with me, and told me to go home. I started with the intention of going to the house; but, in attempting to cross the fence out of the field where we were, my strength entirely failed me, and I fell helpless on the ground, and for a time was quite unconscious of anything.

"The first thing that I can recollect was a voice speaking unto me, calling me by name. I looked up, and beheld the same messenger standing over my head, surrounded by light as before. He then again related unto me all that he had related to me the previous night, and commanded me to go to my father and tell him of the vision and commandments which I had received.

"I obeyed; I returned to my father in the field, and rehearsed the whole matter to him. He replied to me that it was of God, and told me to go and do as commanded by the messenger. I left the field, and went to the place where the messenger had told me the plates were deposited; and owing to the distinctness of the vision which I had had concerning it, I knew the place the instant that I arrived there.

"Convenient to the village of Manchester, Ontario county, New York, stands a hill of considerable size, and the most elevated of any in the neighborhood. On the west side of this hill, not far from the top, under a stone of considerable size, lay the plates, deposited in a stone box. This stone was thick and rounding in the middle on the upper side, and thinner towards the edges, so that the middle part of it was visible above the ground, but the edge all around was covered with earth.

"Having removed the earth, I obtained a lever, which I got fixed under the edge of the stone, and with a little exertion raised it up. I looked in, and there indeed did I behold the plates, the Urim and Thummim, and the breastplate, as stated by the messenger. The box in which they lay was formed by laying stones together in some kind of cement. In the bottom of the box were laid two stones crossways of the box, and on these stones lay the plates and the other things with them.

"I made an attempt to take them out, but was forbidden by the messenger, and was again informed that the time for bringing them forth had not yet arrived, neither would it, until four years from that time; but he told me that I should come to that place precisely in one year from that time, and that he would there meet with me, and that I should continue to do so until the time should come for obtaining the plates.

"Accordingly, as I had been commanded, I went at the end of each year, and at each time I found the same messenger there, and received instruction and intelligence from him at each of our interviews, respecting what the Lord was going to do, and how and in what manner His kingdom was to be conducted in the last days.

* * * * * * *

"At length the time arrived for obtaining the plates, the Urim and Thummim, and the breastplate. On the twenty-second day of September, one thousand eight hundred and twenty-seven, having gone as usual at the end of another year to the place where they were deposited, the same heavenly messenger delivered them up to me with this charge: That I should be responsible for them; that if I should let them go carelessly, or through any neglect of mine, I should be cut off; but that if I would use all my endeavors to preserve them, until he, the messenger, should call for them, they should be protected.

"I soon found out the reason why I had received such strict charges to keep them safe, and why it was that the messenger had said that when I had done what was required at my hand, he would call for them. For no sooner was it known that I had them, than the most strenuous exertions were used to get them from me. Every stratagem that could be invented was resorted to for that purpose. The persecution became more bitter and severe than before, and multitudes were on the alert continually to get them from me if possible. But by the wisdom of God, they remained safe in my hands, until I had accomplished by them what was required at my hand. When, according to arrangements, the messenger called for them, I delivered them up to him; and he has them in his charge until this day, being the second day of May, one thousand eight hundred and thirty-eight."

For the complete record, see Joseph Smith—History, in the Pearl of Great Price, and History of The Church of Jesus Christ of Latter-day Saints, volume 1, chapters 1 through 6.

The ancient record thus brought forth from the earth as the voice of a people speaking from the dust, and translated into modern speech by the gift and power of God as attested by Divine affirmation, was first published to the world in the year 1830 as THE BOOK OF MORMON.

A BRIEF EXPLANATION ABOUT THE BOOK OF MORMON

The Book of Mormon is a sacred record of peoples in ancient America, and was engraved upon sheets of metal. Four kinds of metal record plates are spoken of in the book itself

1. The Plates *of Nephi*, which were of two kinds: the Small Plates and the Large Plates. The former were more particularly devoted to the spiritual matters and the ministry and teachings of the prophets, while the latter were occupied mostly by a secular history of the peoples concerned (1 Nephi 9: 2-4). From the time of Mosiah, however, the large plates also included items of major spiritual importance.

2. The Plates of Mormon, which consist of an abridgment by Mormon from the Large Plates of Nephi, with many commentaries. These plates also contained a continuation of the history by Mormon and additions by his son Moroni.

3. *The Plates of Ether*, which present a history of the Jaredites. This record was abridged by Moroni, who inserted comments of his own and incorporated the record with the general history under the title "Book of Ether."

4. *The Plates of Brass* brought by the people of Lehi from Jerusalem in 600 B.C. These contained "the five books of Moses, . . . And also a record of the Jews from the beginning, . . . down to the commencement of the reign of Zedekiah, king of Judah; And also the prophecies of the holy prophets" (1 Nephi 5: 11-13). Many quotations from these plates, citing Isaiah and other biblical and nonbiblical prophets, appear in the Book of Mormon.

The Book of Mormon comprises fifteen main parts or divisions, known, with one exception, as books, each designated by the name of its principal author. The first portion (the first six books, ending with Omni) is a translation from the Small Plates of Nephi. Between books of Omni and Mosiah is an insert called The Words of Mormon. This insert connects the record engraved on the Small Plates with Mormon's abridgment of the Large Plates.

The longest portion, from Mosiah to Mormon, chapter 7, inclusive, is a translation of Mormon's abridgment of the Large Plates of Nephi. The concluding portion, from Mormon, chapter 8, to the end to the volume, was engraved by Mormon's son Moroni, who, after finishing the record of his father's life, made an abridgment of the Jaredite record (as the Book of Ether) and later added the parts known as the Book of Moroni.

In or about the year A.D. 421, Moroni, the last of the Nephite prophet-historians, sealed the sacred record and hid it up unto the Lord, to be brought forth in the latter days, as predicted by the voice of God through his ancient prophets. In A.D. 1823, this same Moroni, then a

> resurrected personage, visited the Prophet Joseph Smith and subsequently delivered the engraved plates to him.
>
> About this edition: Some minor errors in the text have been perpetuated in past editions of the Book of Mormon. This edition contains corrections that seem appropriate to bring the material into conformity with prepublication manuscripts and early editions edited by the Prophet Joseph Smith.

The Book of Mormon claims to be another witness that Jesus Christ really lived, that He was and is God's Son. It claims to contain the writings of ancient prophets. One of these prophets lead a small group of people from Jerusalem to the American continent around 600 B.C.

God continued to call prophets among these people. The Book of Mormon is a collection of the writings of these prophets and record keepers. It is named after Mormon, one of the last of these ancient prophets.

These prophets knew about God's plan for His children and the mission of Jesus Christ. They recorded that Christ appeared, after His Resurrection, to the people in America, taught them His gospel, and formed His Church among them. The book claims to contain the teaching of Jesus Christ, testifying of His atonement and His love.

A messenger of God, named Moroni, told Joseph Smith, by eight revelations, where to find gold plates that was the history of the people that lived in America. Latter Day Saints (LDS) believe these people are the ten lost tribes of Israel.

The Book of Mormon claims to be more correct than the Bible (Introduction to the Book of Mormon; History of the Church 4:461).

However, the Book of Mormon has had changes in the area of doctrine where the copyist errors in the ancient manuscripts of the Bible do not affect doctrine. Further, The Book of Mormon should not have needed any changes ever. If God inspired the original copy then it would be without error. Since the invention of the printing press, there would be no need for copyist, therefore no human error in copying should occur.

The Book of Mormon does not contain LDS doctrine. It is more Christian than it is Mormon. LDS doctrine, as taught later in other LDS writings, is about many gods, god being a man, men and women potentially becoming gods, but the Book of Mormon is basically Christian in its teachings.

The following information is in the Book of Mormon. Compare it to Mormon doctrine and see the differences. It is obvious that Mormonism grew and was pasted together as it developed. It is not internally consistent and it is self-contradictory.

The Book of Mormon Versus Mormon Doctrine

The Book of Mormon	Mormon Doctrine
There is only one God. *Mosiah 15:1,5; Alma 11:28; 2 Nephi 31:21*	**Mormonism teaches there are many gods.** *D&C 132:19-20; Joseph Smith, Journal of Discourses, Vol. 6, p. 5*
The Trinity is one God. *Alma 11:44; Mosiah 15:5; 2 Nephi 31:21*	**The Trinity is three separate gods.** *James Talmage, Articles of Faith, p. 35. 1985.*
God is unchanging. *Mormon 9:9,19; Moroni 8:18; Alma 41:8; 3 Nephi 24:6*	**God is increasing in knowledge.** *Joseph Smith, Journal of Discourses, Vol. 6, p. 120.*
God is spirit. *Alma 18:24,28; 22:9,11*	**God has the form of a man.** *Joseph Smith, Journal of Discourses, Vol. 6, p. 3.*
Eternal hell. *Jacob 3:11; 6:10; 2 Nephi 19:16; 28:21-23.*	**Hell is not eternal.** *James Talmage, Articles of Faith, p. 55.*
Polygamy condemned. *Jacob 1:15; 2:23,24,27,31;3:5; Mosiah 11:2,4; Ether 10:5,7*	**Polygamy was taught and practiced.** *Brigham Young, Journal of Discourses, Vol. 3, p. 266*

12 Essential Mormon Doctrines not Found in the Book of Mormon

If the Book of Mormon is the "most correct book of any on earth" (History of the Church, vol. 4:461), then why does it not contain essential LDS doctrines such as ...

1. Church organization

2. Plurality of Gods

3. Plurality of wives doctrine

4. Word of Wisdom

5. God is an exalted man

6. Celestial marriage

7. Men may become Gods

8. Three degrees of glory

9. Baptism for the dead

10. Eternal progression

11. The Aaronic Priesthood

12. Melchizedek Priesthood

Doctrine and Covenants

The following are the opening pages to the Doctrine and Covenants. They provide a good understanding of the LDS view of the Doctrine and Covenants, its creation and beliefs foundation to LDS doctrines.

> EXPLANATORY INTRODUCTION
>
> The Doctrine and Covenants is a collection of divine revelations and inspired declarations given for the establishment and regulation of the kingdom of God on the

earth in the last days. Although most of the sections are directed to members of The Church of Jesus Christ of Latter-day Saints, the messages, warnings, and exhortations are for the benefit of all mankind, and contain an invitation to all people everywhere to hear the voice of the Lord Jesus Christ, speaking to them for their temporal well-being and their everlasting salvation.

Most of the revelations in this compilation were received through Joseph Smith, Jun., the first prophet and president of The Church of Jesus Christ of Latter-day Saints. Others were issued through some of his successors in the Presidency. (See headings to Sections 135, 136, and 138, and Official Declarations 1 and 2.)

The book of Doctrine and Covenants is one of the standard works of the Church in company with the Holy Bible, the Book of Mormon, and the Pearl of Great Price. However, the Doctrine and Covenants is unique because it is not a translation of an ancient document, but is of modern origin and was given of God through his chosen prophets for the restoration of his holy work and the establishment of the kingdom of God on the earth in these days. In the revelations one hears the tender but firm voice of the Lord Jesus Christ, speaking anew in the dispensation of the fullness of times; and the work that is initiated herein is preparatory to his second coming, in fulfillment of and in concert with the words of all the holy prophets since the world began.

Joseph Smith, Jun., was born December 23, 1805, in Sharon, Windsor County, Vermont. During his early life he moved with his family to Manchester, in western New York. It was while he was living near Manchester in the spring of 1820, when he was fourteen years of age, that he experienced his first vision, in which he was visited in person by God, the Eternal Father, and his Son Jesus Christ. He was told in this vision that the true Church of Jesus Christ that had been established in New Testament times, and which had administered the fullness of the gospel, was no longer on the earth. Other divine manifestations followed in which he was taught by many angels; it was shown to him that God had a special work for him to do on the earth, and that through him the Church of Jesus Christ would be restored to the earth.

In the course of time Joseph Smith was enabled by divine assistance to translate and publish the Book of Mormon. In the meantime he and Oliver Cowdery were ordained to the Aaronic Priesthood by John the Baptist in May 1829 (D&C 13), and soon thereafter they were also ordained to the Melchizedek Priesthood by the ancient apostles Peter, James, and John (D&C 27: 12). Other ordinations followed in which priesthood keys were conferred upon them by Moses, Elijah, Elias, and many ancient prophets (D&C 110; 128: 18, 21). These ordinations were, in fact, a restoration of divine authority to man on the earth. On April 6, 1830, under heavenly direction, the Prophet Joseph Smith organized the Church, and thus the true Church of Jesus Christ is once again operative as an institution among men, with authority to teach the gospel and administer the ordinances of salvation. (See Pearl of Great Price, Joseph Smith—History 1: 1-75; D&C 20.)

These sacred revelations were received in answer to prayer, in times of need, and came out of real-life situations involving real people. The Prophet and his associates sought for divine guidance, and these revelations certify that they received it. In the revelations one sees the restoration and unfolding of the gospel of Jesus Christ and the ushering in of the dispensation of the fullness of times. The westward movement of the Church from New York and Pennsylvania, to Ohio, to Missouri, to Illinois, and finally to the Great Basin of western America, and the mighty struggles of the saints in attempting to build Zion on the earth in modern times, are also shown forth in these revelations.

Several of the earlier sections involve matters regarding the translation and publication of the Book of Mormon (see Sections 3, 5, 10, 17, 19). Some later sections reflect the work of the Prophet Joseph Smith in making an inspired translation of the Bible, during which many of the great doctrinal sections were received (see, for example,

Sections 37, 45, 73, 76, 77, 86, 91, and 132, each of which has some direct relationship to the Bible translation).

In the revelations the doctrines of the gospel are set forth with explanations about such fundamental matters as the nature of the Godhead, the origin of man, the reality of Satan, the purpose of mortality, the necessity for obedience, the need for repentance, the workings of the Holy Spirit, the ordinances and performances that pertain to salvation, the destiny of the earth, the future conditions of man after the resurrection and the judgment, the eternity of the marriage relationship, and the eternal nature of the family. Likewise the gradual unfolding of the administrative structure of the Church is shown with the calling of bishops, the First Presidency, the Council of Twelve, and the Seventy, and the establishment of other presiding offices and quorums. Finally, the testimony that is given of Jesus Christ—his divinity, his majesty, his perfection, his love, and his redeeming power—makes this book of great value to the human family and of more worth than the riches of the whole earth.

A number of the revelations were published in Zion (Independence), Missouri, in 1833, under the title A Book of Commandments for the Government of the Church of Christ. Concerning this publication the elders of the Church gave solemn testimony that the Lord had borne record to their souls that these revelations were true. As the Lord continued to communicate with his servants, an enlarged compilation was published two years later in Kirtland, Ohio, with the title Doctrine and Covenants of the Church of the Latter Day Saints. To this publication in 1835, the written testimony of the Twelve Apostles was attached as follows

TESTIMONY OF THE TWELVE APOSTLES TO THE TRUTH OF THE BOOK OF DOCTRINE AND COVENANTS

The Testimony of the Witnesses to the Book of the Lord's Commandments, which commandments He gave to His Church through Joseph Smith, Jun., who was appointed by the voice of the Church for this purpose:

We, therefore, feel willing to bear testimony to all the world of mankind, to every creature upon the face of the earth, that the Lord has borne record to our souls, through the Holy Ghost shed forth upon us, that these commandments were given by inspiration of God, and are profitable for all men and are verily true.

We give this testimony unto the world, the Lord being our helper; and it is through the grace of God the Father, and His Son, Jesus Christ, that we are permitted to have this privilege of bearing this testimony unto the world, in the which we rejoice exceedingly, praying the Lord always that the children of men may be profited thereby.

The names of the Twelve were

Thomas B. Marsh
David W. Patten
Brigham Young
Heber C. Kimball
Orson Hyde
Wm. E. McLellin
Parley P. Pratt
Luke S. Johnson
William Smith
Orson Pratt
John F. Boynton
Lyman E. Johnson

In successive editions of the Doctrine and Covenants, additional revelations or other matters of record have been added, as received, and as accepted by competent assemblies or conferences of the Church.

Beginning with the 1835 edition a series of seven theological lessons was also included; these were titled the "Lectures on Faith." These had been prepared for use in the School of the Prophets in Kirtland, Ohio, in 1834-1835. Although profitable for doctrine and instruction, these lectures have been omitted from the Doctrine and Covenants since the 1921 edition because they were not given or presented as revelations to the whole Church.

> In the current edition of the Doctrine and Covenants three documents have been included for the first time. These are Sections 137 and 138, setting forth the fundamentals of salvation for the dead; and Official Declaration 2, announcing that all worthy male members of the Church may be ordained to the priesthood without regard for race or color.
>
> It is evident that some errors have been perpetuated in past editions, particularly in the historical portions of the section headings. Consequently this edition contains corrections of dates and place names and also a few other minor corrections when it seemed appropriate (such as discontinuing the unusual names beginning with Section 78). These changes have been made so as to bring the material into conformity with the historical documents. Other special features of this latest edition include maps showing the major geographical locations in which the revelations were received, plus improvements in cross references, section headings, and subject-matter summaries, all of which are designed to help readers to understand and rejoice in the message of the Lord as given in the Doctrine and Covenants.

The Doctrine and Covenants claims to be a collection of divine revelations and inspired declarations given for the establishment and regulation of the kingdom of God on the earth in the last days. The book of Doctrine and Covenants is one of the standard works of LDS. However, the Doctrine and Covenants is unique because it does not claim to be a translation of an ancient document, but is of modern origin and claims to be given of God through chosen prophets for the restoration of his holy work and the establishment of the kingdom of God on the earth in these days.

In the introduction of the latest edition of Doctrine and Covenants, it clearly states that there were additions and more importantly, corrections. Again, if God inspired it in this modern age of the printing press, then there would be no need to correct it. However, some of the changes are due to cultural changes, i.e. the accepting of blacks to the priesthood. This would naturally lead someone to conclude that the LDS God changes.

Pearl of Great Price

The following are the opening pages to the Pearl of Great Price. They provide a good understanding of the LDS view of the Pearl of Great Price, its creation and beliefs foundation to LDS doctrines.

> INTRODUCTORY NOTE
>
> The Pearl of Great Price is a selection of choice materials touching many significant aspects of the faith and doctrine of The Church of Jesus Christ of Latter-day Saints. These items were produced by the Prophet Joseph Smith and were published in the Church periodicals of his day.
>
> The first collection of materials carrying the title Pearl of Great Price was made in 1851 by Elder Franklin D. Richards, then a member of the Council of the Twelve and president of the British Mission. Its purpose was to make more readily accessible some important articles that had had limited circulation in the time of Joseph Smith. As Church membership increased throughout Europe and America there was a need to make these items available. The Pearl of Great Price received wide use and subsequently became a standard work of the Church by action of the First Presidency and the general conference in Salt Lake City on October 10, 1880.
>
> Several revisions have been made in the contents as the needs of the Church have required. In 1878 portions of the Book of Moses not contained in the first edition were added. In 1902 certain parts of the Pearl of Great Price that duplicated material also published in the Doctrine and Covenants were omitted. Arrangement into chapters and verses, with footnotes, was done in 1902. The first publication in double-column pages, with index, was in 1921. No other changes were made until April 1976, when two items of revelation were added. In 1979 these two items were removed from the Pearl of Great Price and placed in the Doctrine and Covenants, where they now appear as Sections 137 and 138. In the present edition

some changes have been made to bring the text into conformity with earlier documents.

Following is a brief introduction to the present contents:

Selections from the Book of Moses. An extract from the book of Genesis of Joseph Smith's Translation of the Bible, which he began in June 1830. See History of the Church, vol. 1, pp. 98-101, 131-139.

The Book of Abraham. A translation from some Egyptian papyri that came into the hands of Joseph Smith in 1835, containing writings of the patriarch Abraham. The translation was published serially in the Times and Seasons beginning March 1, 1842, at Nauvoo, Illinois. See History of the Church, vol. 4, pp. 519-534.

Joseph Smith—Matthew. An extract from the testimony of Matthew in Joseph Smith's Translation of the Bible. See Doctrine and Covenants 45: 60-61 for the divine injunction to begin the translation of the New Testament.

Joseph Smith—History. Excerpts from Joseph Smith's official testimony and history, which he prepared in 1838, and which was published serially in the Times and Seasons in Nauvoo, Illinois, beginning on March 15, 1842. See History of the Church, vol. 1, pp. 1-44, for the complete account.

The Articles of Faith of The Church of Jesus Christ of Latter-day Saints. A statement by Joseph Smith published in the Times and Seasons March 1, 1842, in company with a short history of the Church that was popularly known as the Wentworth Letter. See History of the Church, vol. 4, pp. 535-541.

The Pearl of Great Price is a selection of choice materials touching many significant aspects of the faith and doctrine of LDS. These items produced by Joseph Smith, were published in the Church periodicals of his day.

Church of Jesus Christ of Latter Day Saints

The Church of Jesus Christ of Latter-day Saints state that it is "the only true and living church upon the face of the whole earth" (D&C 1:30)

The Church of Jesus Christ of Latter-day Saints states that when Jesus Christ lived on the earth, He organized His Church so that all people could receive His gospel and return one day to live with God. After Jesus Christ ascended to heaven, His Apostles continued to receive revelation from Him on how to direct the work of His Church. However, after they were killed, members changed the teachings of the Church that He had established. While many good people and some truth remained, this Apostasy, or general falling away from the truth, brought about the withdrawal of the Church from the earth.

They believe that the Apostle Peter prophesied that Jesus would restore His Church before His Second Coming (Acts 3:19–21). In addition, that Jesus Christ began to restore His Church in its fullness to the earth through Joseph Smith in 1820.

It has grown to become a worldwide organization with over 11 million members. It also, was one of the fastest growing religions.

The following is a chart of the hierarchy of The Church of Jesus Christ of Latter-day Saints.

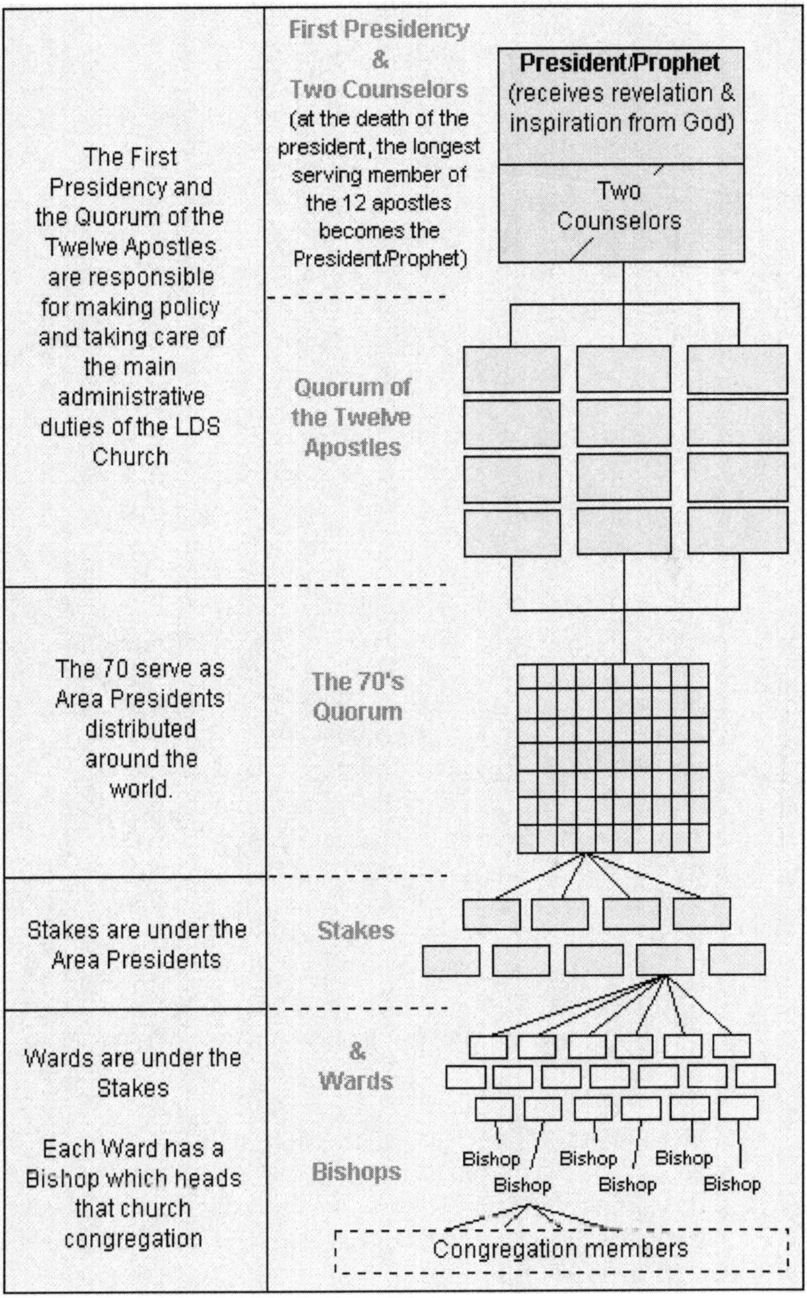
The First Presidency and the Quorum of the Twelve Apostles are responsible for making policy and taking care of the main administrative duties of the LDS Church
First Presidency & Two Counselors
(at the death of the president, the longest serving member of the 12 apostles becomes the President/Prophet)
President/Prophet
(receives revelation & inspiration from God)
Two Counselors
Quorum of the Twelve Apostles
The 70 serve as Area Presidents distributed around the world.
The 70's Quorum
Stakes are under the Area Presidents
Stakes
Wards are under the Stakes
Each Ward has a Bishop which heads that church congregation
& Wards
Bishops
Bishop
Bishop
Bishop
Bishop
Bishop
Bishop
Congregation members

God

Godhead

The LDS do not accept the term Trinity. Their view of the Godhead would be two physical Persons and one Spirit in one Godhead. Therefore, they could claim three persons in one Godhead, however, two of those persons have a physical body. Genesis 1:26-28 is taken literally to mean the God has a physical image and that humanity is created in it. They believe that God is a glorified being of flesh and bones—not just a spirit essence.

> "The Father has a body of flesh and bones as tangible as man's; the Son also; but the Holy Ghost has not a body of flesh and bones, but is a personage of Spirit." (D&C 130:22.)
>
> The Church of Jesus Christ of Latter-day Saints worships a God and a Jesus Christ with bodies, with parts, and with passions. The belief that God has no body, parts, and passions is not a doctrine of Jesus Christ or a doctrine of the holy scriptures but is a doctrine of men, and to worship such a God is in vain. The message of The Church of Jesus Christ of Latter-day Saints to the people of the world is that God the Eternal Father and Jesus Christ live, that they are personages with immortal bodies of flesh and bones and passions, and that all mankind are children of God and are created in his image and likeness, and that Jesus Christ through his Prophet Joseph Smith restored his church with all of his doctrines, commandments, and ordinances as recorded in all of his holy scriptures. (The LDS website)
>
> And he hath brought to pass the redemption of the world, whereby he that is found guiltless before him at the judgment day hath it given unto him to dwell in the presence of God in his kingdom, to sing ceaseless praises with the choirs above, unto the Father, and unto the Son, and unto the Holy Ghost, which are one God, in a state of happiness which hath no end. (Mormon 7:7)

Addressing the issue that Jesus states that the Father is a Spirit in John 4:24 (KJV), Joseph Smith states, “For unto such hath God promised his Spirit. And they who worship him, must worship in spirit and in truth.” (JST, John 4:24.)

They seem to believe that Christians believe that Jesus is a spirit only. In order to prove that the Father has a physical body they prove that Jesus has a body and then apply that to the Father. The Father and Son are separate. Jesus had and has a physical body, but the Father does not. The Father is a spirit (John 4:24).

Joseph Smith saw a confirmation of what Jesus had impressed upon Philip long ago: “Have I been so long time with you, and yet hast thou not known me, Philip? he that hath seen me hath seen the Father; and how sayest thou then, Shew us the Father?” (John 14:9) They state that Jesus was apparently informing his disciples that he and his Father were alike in attributes, in power, and in bodily appearance.

> And now, behold, my beloved brethren, this is the way; and there is none other way nor name given under heaven whereby man can be saved in the kingdom of God. And now, behold, this is the doctrine of Christ, and the only and true doctrine of the Father, and of the Son, and of the Holy Ghost, which is one God, without end. Amen. (2 Nephi 31:21)
>
> AND now Abinadi said unto them: I would that ye should understand that God himself shall come down among the children of men, and shall redeem his people. And because he dwelleth in flesh he shall be called the Son of God, and having subjected the flesh to the will of the Father, being the Father and the Son—The Father, because he was conceived by the power of God; and the Son, because of the flesh; thus becoming the Father and Son—And they are one God, yea, the very Eternal Father of heaven and of earth. (Mosiah 15:1-4)
>
> And Zeezrom said unto him: Thou sayest there is a true and living God? And Amulek said: Yea, there is a true and living God. Now Zeezrom said: Is there more than one God? And he answered, No. … Now, this restoration shall

> come to all, both old and young, both bond and free, both male and female, both the wicked and the righteous; and even there shall not so much as a hair of their heads be lost; but every thing shall be restored to its perfect frame, as it is now, or in the body, and shall be brought and be arraigned before the bar of Christ the Son, and God the Father, and the Holy Spirit, which is one Eternal God, to be judged according to their works, whether they be good or whether they be evil. (Alma 11:26-29, 44)

Lives Near Kolob

LDS doctrine teaches that God used to be a man on another planet, that He became God by following the laws and ordinances of that god on that world, and that He brought one of His wives to this world with whom He produces spirit children who then inhabit human bodies at birth. The first spirit child to be born was Jesus. Second was Satan, and then we all followed. The LDS Jesus is definitely not the same Jesus of the Bible.

LDS state that Abraham says that according to "the Lord's time" a day is "one thousand years" long. This is "one revolution … of Kolob," he says, and it is after the Lord's "manner of reckoning."

> "And the Lord said unto me, by the Urim and Thummim, that Kolob was after the manner of the Lord, according to it's a times and seasons in the revolutions thereof; that one revolution was a day unto the Lord, after his manner of reckoning, it being one thousand years according to the time appointed unto that whereon thou standest. This is the reckoning of the Lord's time, according to the reckoning of Kolob" (Abr. 3:4.)

A FACSIMILE FROM THE BOOK OF ABRAHAM No. 2

EXPLANATION

Fig. 1. Kolob, signifying the first creation, nearest to the celestial, or the residence of God. First in government, the last pertaining to the measurement of time. The measurement according to celestial time, which celestial time signifies one day to a cubit. One day in Kolob is equal to a thousand years according to the measurement of this earth, which is called by the Egyptians Jah-oh-eh.

Fig. 2. Stands next to Kolob, called by the Egyptians Oliblish, which is the next grand governing creation near to the celestial or the place where God resides; holding the key of power also, pertaining to other planets; as revealed from God to Abraham, as he offered sacrifice upon an altar, which he had built unto the Lord.

Fig. 3. Is made to represent God, sitting upon his throne, clothed with power and authority; with a crown of eternal light upon his head; representing also the grand Key-words of the Holy Priesthood, as revealed to Adam in the Garden of Eden, as also to Seth, Noah, Melchizedek, Abraham, and all to whom the Priesthood was revealed.

Fig. 4. Answers to the Hebrew word Raukeeyang, signifying expanse, or the firmament of the heavens; also a numerical figure, in Egyptian signifying one thousand; answering to the measuring of the time of Oliblish, which is equal with Kolob in its revolution and in its measuring of time.

Fig. 5. Is called in Egyptian Enish-go-on-dosh; this is one of the governing planets also, and is said by the Egyptians to be the Sun, and to borrow its light from Kolob through the medium of Kae-e-vanrash, which is the grand Key, or, in other words, the governing power, which governs fifteen other fixed planets or stars, as also Floeese or the Moon, the Earth and the Sun in their annual revolutions. This planet receives its power through the medium of Kli-flos-is-es, or Hah-ko-kau-beam, the stars represented by numbers 22 and 23, receiving light from the revolutions of Kolob.

Fig. 6. Represents this earth in its four quarters.

Fig. 7. Represents God sitting upon his throne, revealing through the heavens the grand Key-words of the Priesthood; as, also, the sign of the Holy Ghost unto Abraham, in the form of a dove.

Fig. 8. Contains writings that cannot be revealed unto the world; but is to be had in the Holy Temple of God.

Fig. 9. Ought not to be revealed at the present time.

Fig. 10. Also.

> Fig. 11. Also. If the world can find out these numbers, so let it be. Amen.
>
> Figures 12, 13, 14, 15, 16, 17, 18, 19, 20, and 21 will be given in the own due time of the Lord.

The above translation is given as far as we have any right to give at the present time.

Jesus Christ

Deity

They do not believe in the dual nature of Jesus, being both fully God and fully man. Jesus was God became man, died and became God again. Christ is now fully God, but subordinate to his Father. Jesus is Jehovah of the Old Testament.

> AND now Abinadi said unto them: I would that ye should understand that God himself shall come down among the children of men, and shall redeem his people. And because he dwelleth in flesh he shall be called the Son of God, and having subjected the flesh to the will of the Father, being the Father and the Son—The Father, because he was conceived by the power of God; and the Son, because of the flesh; thus becoming the Father and Son—And they are one God, yea, the very Eternal Father of heaven and of earth. (Mosiah 15:1-4)
>
> Wherefore, the Almighty God gave his Only Begotten Son, as it is written in those scriptures which have been given of him. He suffered temptations but gave no heed unto them. He was crucified, died, and rose again the third day; And ascended into heaven, to sit down on the right hand of the Father, to reign with almighty power according to the will of the Father; That as many as would believe and be baptized in his holy name, and endure in faith to the end, should be saved—Not only those who believed after he came in the meridian of time, in the flesh, but all those from the beginning, even as many as were before he came, who believed in the words of the holy prophets, who spake

> as they were inspired by the gift of the Holy Ghost, who truly testified of him in all things, should have eternal life, As well as those who should come after, who should believe in the gifts and callings of God by the Holy Ghost, which beareth record of the Father and of the Son; Which Father, Son, and Holy Ghost are one God, infinite and eternal, without end. Amen. (D&C 20:21-28)

Born of a Virgin

LDS believe Jesus was born of a virgin. Mary was in some unspecified manner made pregnant by God the Father, through the power of the Holy Spirit. Hence Jesus is not a metaphorical Son, but a begotten Son. Jesus is not the son of the Holy Spirit, but of the Father through the Holy Spirit.

> And behold, he shall be born of Mary, at Jerusalem which is the land of our forefathers, she being a virgin, a precious and chosen vessel, who shall be overshadowed and conceive by the power of the Holy Ghost, and bring forth a son, yea, even the Son of God. (Alma 7:10)

> And it came to pass that I looked and beheld the great city of Jerusalem, and also other cities. And I beheld the city of Nazareth; and in the city of Nazareth I beheld a virgin, and she was exceedingly fair and white. And it came to pass that I saw the heavens open; and an angel came down and stood before me; and he said unto me: Nephi, what beholdest thou? And I said unto him: A virgin, most beautiful and fair above all other virgins. And he said unto me: Knowest thou the condescension of God? And I said unto him: I know that he loveth his children; nevertheless, I do not know the meaning of all things. And he said unto me: Behold, the virgin whom thou seest is the mother of the Son of God, after the manner of the flesh. And it came to pass that I beheld that she was carried away in the Spirit; and after she had been carried away in the Spirit for the space of a time the angel spake unto me, saying: Look! And I looked and beheld the virgin again, bearing a child in her arms. (1 Nephi 11:13-20)

Other beliefs about Jesus are found in a book call Mormon Doctrine. This book is not an authority, however, the author is one of their Quorum of Twelve, and thus an authority himself. Some LDS may dispute these teachings, but many will not.

- The first spirit to be born in heaven was Jesus (Mormon Doctrine, page 129).
- The Devil was born as a spirit after Jesus "in the morning of pre-existence," (Mormon Doctrine, page 192).
- Jesus and Satan are spirit brothers and we were all born as siblings in heaven to them both, (Mormon Doctrine, p. 163).
- A plan of salvation was needed for the people of earth so Jesus offered a plan to the father and Satan offered a plan to the father but Jesus' plan was accepted. In effect the Devil wanted to be the Saviour of all Mankind and to "deny men their agency and to dethrone god." (Mormon Doctrine, page 193; Journal of Discourses, vol. 6, page 8).
- God had sexual relations with Mary to make the body of Jesus, (Brigham Young, Journal of Discourses, Vol. 4, p. 218, 1857; vol. 8, p. 115).—This one is disputed among many Mormons and not always 'officially' taught and believed. Nevertheless, Young, the 2nd prophet of the Mormon church taught it.

Sin

LDS believe that men will be punished for their own sins, and not for Adam's transgression. Thus, there is not a belief in original sin. The basis of this argument is that the spirit of man was created prior to the fall and is good.

Pre-existence

LDS doctrine teaches that God created man as spirits before the sixth day of creation. The life you lived as a spirit determines the life you will have on earth with a body. However, no one has any knowledge of his or her life before birth. LDS believe that you did not suddenly spring into existence the moment you were born.

> Man was also in the beginning with God. Intelligence, or the light of truth, was not created or made, neither indeed can be. (D&C 93:29)

LDS teach that you were happy in God's presence, but He knew that you needed more in order to progress. You did not have a physical body like you do now, and you needed a chance to gain experience on your own—away from God's presence, but with the ability to communicate with Him and receive help. So He sent you to Earth, hoping that you would return to Him and receive everything He has to offer you.

Freewill

LDS believe that one of the most precious gifts God has given people is the ability and power to make choices. God respects a person's freedom to choose. He will never force anyone to choose good, nor will He stop anyone from making wrong choices. He knows that by making choices and experiencing their consequences, you learn the difference between good and evil. As you learn to choose good, you find greater happiness.

Children of God

Man is the literal, physical offspring of God (Acts 17:28-29). LDS believe that everyone is a child of God with a divine nature and a divine destiny. You lived with Him as a spirit before you were born. God sent you to Earth to receive a body and gain the experiences you need to return to Him.

> And now, because of the covenant which ye have made ye shall be called the children of Christ, his sons, and his daughters; for behold, this day he hath spiritually begotten you; for ye say that your hearts are changed through faith on his name; therefore, ye are born of him and have become his sons and his daughters. (Mosiah 5:7)

The Fall was a joy for man because it brought mortality and physical death.

> Adam fell that men might be; and men care, that they might have joy. (2 Nephi 2:25)

Salvation

A Different Gospel

LDS state that they believe in salvation through Jesus Christ.

> And moreover, I say unto you, that there shall be no other name given nor any other way nor means whereby salvation can come unto the children of men, only in and through the name of Christ, the Lord Omnipotent. (Mosiah 3:17)

> And now, behold, my beloved brethren, this is the way; and there is none other way nor name given under heaven whereby man can be saved in the kingdom of God. And now, behold, this is the doctrine of Christ, and the only and true doctrine of the Father, and of the Son, and of the Holy Ghost, which is one God, without end. Amen. (2 Nephi 31:21)

> I glory in plainness; I glory in truth; I glory in my Jesus, for he hath redeemed my soul from hell. (2 Nephi 33:6)

> And men are instructed sufficiently that they know good from evil. And the law is given unto men. And by the law no flesh is justified; or, by the law men are cut off. Yea, by the temporal law they were cut off; and also, by the spiritual law they perish from that which is good, and become miserable forever. Wherefore, redemption cometh in and through the Holy Messiah; for he is full of grace and truth. Behold, he offereth himself a sacrifice for sin, to answer the ends of the law, unto all those who have a broken heart and a contrite spirit; and unto none else can the ends of the law be answered. Wherefore, how great the importance to make these things known unto the inhabitants of the earth, that they may know that there is no flesh that can dwell in the presence of God, save it be through the merits, and mercy, and grace of the Holy

> Messiah, who layeth down his life according to the flesh, and taketh it again by the power of the Spirit, that he may bring to pass the resurrection of the dead, being the first that should rise. (2 Nephi 2:5-8)

> And after that he came men also were saved by faith in his name; and by faith, they become the sons of God. And as surely as Christ liveth he spake these words unto our fathers, saying: Whatsoever thing ye shall ask the Father in my name, which is good, in faith believing that ye shall receive, behold, it shall be done unto you. (Moroni 7:26)

However, the LDS church believes in a different gospel then that taught in the Bible as evidenced by the fact that they claim the Book of Mormon restores the gospel and contains the fullness of the gospel. This means that the fullness of the gospel was lost and claims to have been taught to Adam, Enoch, Noah, Abraham and many others.

However, if Adam, Enoch, Noah, Abraham and many others lost this “fullness of the gospel” and it had to continue to be taught over and over again, how can we trust that Joseph Smith is the first to get it right and keep it right? Furthermore, what does that teach about God that He cannot or does not keep the “fullness of the gospel” protected through the centuries? LDS doctrine states that God wants all His children to know the truth, yet He does not protect that truth from error. That does not sound like God sincerely cares for His children.

> Furthermore, there is no salvation without accepting Joseph Smith as a prophet of God, (*Doctrines of Salvation*, Vol. 1, p. 188).

Baptism for the Dead

LDS believe that baptism is necessary for salvation as seen in their teachings on baptism for the dead.

LDS teach that many people have died without receiving baptism and other ordinances that Jesus Christ taught were necessary to enter the kingdom of God (John 3:5). Because God wants all His children to have the opportunity to return to Him, He has provided a way for those who have died without these ordinances to receive them.

In holy temples, members of the Church can perform these ordinances on behalf of their ancestors who have died. This makes it possible for those who have not received these ordinances to accept them, if they choose, and return to live one day with our God.

Salvation by Works Not Grace and Faith Alone

Jesus took upon himself the sins of all men on conditions of repentance, offering all people a general salvation. An additional salvation is an individual salvation and is conditioned not only upon grace, but also upon obedience to gospel law. Perhaps the most famous statement of the LDS understanding of the relation between grace and works is in 2 Nephi 25:23.

> "For we labor diligently to write, to persuade our children, and also our brethren, to believe in Christ, and to be reconciled to God; for we know that it is by grace that we are saved, *after all we can do*." (emphasis added)

LDS believe through the atonement of Christ, all mankind may be saved, by obedience to the laws and ordinances of the gospel. Jesus Christ did what only He could do in atoning for our sins. To make His atonement fully effective in our individual lives, we must have 1) faith in Christ, 2) repent of our sins, 3) be baptized, 4) receive the Holy Ghost, 5) obey His commandments, and 6) strive to become like Him. As we do these things through His atonement, we can return to live with God forever.

The Joseph Smith Translation of James 2:14-21 displays the teaching that salvation comes from faith and works and not faith "being alone" (v.17).

> 14 What profit is it, my brethren, for a man to say he hath faith, and hath not works? can faith save him?
>
> 15 Yea, a man may say, I will show thee I have faith without works; but I say, Show me thy faith without works, and I will show thee my faith by my works.

> 16 For if a brother or sister be naked and destitute, and one of you say, Depart in peace, be warmed and filled; notwithstanding he give not those things which are needful to the body; what profit is your faith unto such?
>
> 17 Even so faith, if it have not works is dead, being alone.
>
> 18 Therefore wilt thou know, O vain man, that faith without works is dead and cannot save you?
>
> 19 Thou believest there is one God; thou doest well; the devils also believe, and tremble; thou hast made thyself like unto them, not being justified.
>
> 20 Was not Abraham our father justified by works, when he had offered Isaac his son upon the altar?
>
> 21 Seest thou how works wrought with his faith, and by works was faith made perfect?

God knew that while you were on Earth you would make mistakes—everyone does. So, as part of His plan, He provided a Savior, Jesus Christ, who would make it possible for sins to be forgiven, and for all people who accept His sacrifice to return to live with Heavenly Father.

LDS believes in salvation through grace by faith, but the faith is meaning the “faithful”.

> And we know that justification through the grace of our Lord and Savior Jesus Christ is just and true; (D&C 20:30)

LDS do not believe in eternal security, thus, one can “fall from grace”. Since works gets you in it must also keep you in and a lack there of causes a loss of salvation. They would be in line with Arminian theology.

> But there is a possibility that man may fall from grace and depart from the living God; (D&C 20:32)

Second Chance

LDS believe the period between death and resurrection is still a probationary or testing period for those in hell. If they repent and turn to Christ, they may yet be redeemed from Satan through the atonement and inherit some degree of glory among the many mansions of the Father. To this end, they believe the gospel is preached to the ignorant and rebellious spirits in prison, that they may repent and accept Christ and live (John 5:25-29; 1 Peter3:18-20; 4:6).

Eternal State

Becoming gods (like Christ)

LDS believe that God ordained and established a plan of salvation whereby his spirit children might advance and progress and become like Him. After you become a LDS, you have the potential of becoming a god (Teachings of the Prophet Joseph Smith, pages 345-347, 354).

According to their formula, "God became man that man might become God." LDS believe that early Christians "were invited to 'study' to become gods" (note the plural).

> And again, verily I say unto you, if a man marry a wife by my word, which is my law, and by the new and everlasting covenant, and it is sealed unto them by the Holy Spirit of promise, by him who is anointed, unto whom I have appointed this power and the keys of this priesthood; and it shall be said unto them—Ye shall come forth in the first resurrection; and if it be after the first resurrection, in the next resurrection; and shall inherit thrones, kingdoms, principalities, and powers, dominions, all heights and depths—then shall it be written in the Lamb's Book of Life, that he shall commit no murder whereby to shed innocent blood, and if ye abide in my covenant, and commit no murder whereby to shed innocent blood, it shall be done unto them in all things whatsoever my servant hath put upon them, in time, and through all eternity; and shall be of full force when they are out of the world; and they shall

> pass by the angels, and the gods, which are set there, to their exaltation and glory in all things, as hath been sealed upon their heads, which glory shall be a fullness and a continuation of the seeds forever and ever. Then shall they be gods, because they have no end; therefore shall they be from everlasting to everlasting, because they continue; then shall they be above all, because all things are subject unto them. Then shall they be gods, because they have all power, and the angels are subject unto them. (D&C 132:19-20)

Although this is the only “scriptural” reference to deification of man, many of the church elders, members of the Quorum of Twelve Apostles and their first prophet Joseph Smith, teach this doctrine. The Quorum of Twelve Apostles have the responsibility for making policy and the President or Prophet is responsible for correctly interpreting the “scriptures”. Therefore, since the Quorum of Twelve Apostles believe and teach this doctrine it is safe to say it is LDS doctrine. The explanation of this doctrine comes from the interpretation of D&C 132:19-20 from those that have the authority in the LDS church to interpret correctly the “scriptures”. They reference the following verse from the Bible to support their argument: Exodus 7:1; Psalm 82:1-6 and John 10:34-36.

They explain their view by stating that even a cursory glance at early Christian thought reveals, the idea that man might become as God—known in Greek as theosis or theopoiesis —may be found virtually everywhere, from the New Testament through the writings of the first four centuries. Church members take seriously such passages as Psalm 82:6 [Ps. 82:6], John 10:33-36, and Philippians 2:5-6 [Philip. 2:5-6], in which a plurality of gods and the idea of becoming like God are mentioned.

Heaven

There are three levels of heaven: telestial, terrestrial, and celestial, (*Mormon Doctrine*, p. 348).

The lowest level is the telestial glory, reserved for those who were wicked in the flesh but who in some sense and to some degree turned to Christ in their suffering between death and resurrection (D&C 76: 81-113).

The next highest level, the terrestrial kingdom, is reserved for the honorable men and women of the earth, the "righteous", who rejected the fullness of the gospel and the witness of the Holy Spirit during their mortal lives but changed their minds in the spirit prison (D&C 76: 71-80). Their lot in eternity is to dwell with Jesus in glory forever, but without enjoying the separate presence of the Father and continuing family relationships.

The highest level is the celestial kingdom, which is reserved for LDS members, children who died before the age of 8 years old, the mental handicapped who have the mind of a child under 8 years old and those good people of every religious belief who never heard and understood the gospel during their lives or who never felt the Spirit bear witness to it (D&C 76: 50-70).

D&C 76:50-113

> 50 And again we bear record—for we saw and heard, and this is the testimony of the gospel of Christ concerning them who shall come forth in the resurrection of the just—
> 51 They are they who received the testimony of Jesus, and believed on his name and were baptized after the manner of his burial, being buried in the water in his name, and this according to the commandment which he has given—
> 52 That by keeping the commandments they might be washed and cleansed from all their sins, and receive the Holy Spirit by the laying on of the hands of him who is ordained and sealed unto this power;
> 53 And who overcome by faith, and are sealed by the Holy Spirit of promise, which the Father sheds forth upon all those who are just and true.
> 54 They are they who are the church of the Firstborn.
> 55 They are they into whose hands the Father has given all things—
> 56 They are they who are priests and kings, who have received of his fullness, and of his glory;
> 57 And are priests of the Most High, after the order of Melchizedek, which was after the order of Enoch, which was after the order of the Only Begotten Son.
> 58 Wherefore, as it is written, they are gods, even the sons of God—
> 59 Wherefore, all things are theirs, whether life or death, or

things present, or things to come, all are theirs and they are Christ's, and Christ is God's.
60 And they shall overcome all things.
61 Wherefore, let no man glory in man, but rather let him glory in God, who shall subdue all enemies under his feet.
62 These shall dwell in the presence of God and his Christ forever and ever.
63 These are they whom he shall bring with him, when he shall come in the clouds of heaven to reign on the earth over his people.
64 These are they who shall have part in the first resurrection.
65 These are they who shall come forth in the resurrection of the just.
66 These are they who are come unto Mount Zion, and unto the city of the living God, the heavenly place, the holiest of all.
67 These are they who have come to an innumerable company of angels, to the general assembly and church of Enoch, and of the Firstborn.
68 These are they whose names are written in heaven, where God and Christ are the judge of all.
69 These are they who are just men made perfect through Jesus the mediator of the new covenant, who wrought out this perfect atonement through the shedding of his own blood.
70 These are they whose bodies are celestial, whose glory is that of the sun, even the glory of God, the highest of all, whose glory the sun of the firmament is written of as being typical.
71 And again, we saw the terrestrial world, and behold and lo, these are they who are of the terrestrial, whose glory differs from that of the church of the Firstborn who have received the fullness of the Father, even as that of the moon differs from the sun in the firmament.
72 Behold, these are they who died without law;
73 And also they who are the spirits of men kept in prison, whom the Son visited, and preached the gospel unto them, that they might be judged according to men in the flesh;
74 Who received not the testimony of Jesus in the flesh, but afterwards received it.
75 These are they who are honorable men of the earth,

who were blinded by the craftiness of men.
76 These are they who receive of his glory, but not of his fullness.
77 These are they who receive of the presence of the Son, but not of the fullness of the Father.
78 Wherefore, they are bodies terrestrial, and not bodies celestial, and differ in glory as the moon differs from the sun.
79 These are they who are not valiant in the testimony of Jesus; wherefore, they obtain not the crown over the kingdom of our God.
80 And now this is the end of the vision which we saw of the terrestrial, that the Lord commanded us to write while we were yet in the Spirit.
81 And again, we saw the glory of the telestial, which glory is that of the lesser, even as the glory of the stars differs from that of the glory of the moon in the firmament.
82 These are they who received not the gospel of Christ, neither the testimony of Jesus.
83 These are they who deny not the Holy Spirit.
84 These are they who are thrust down to hell.
85 These are they who shall not be redeemed from the devil until the last resurrection, until the Lord, even Christ the Lamb, shall have finished his work.
86 These are they who receive not of his fullness in the eternal world, but of the Holy Spirit through the ministration of the terrestrial;
87 And the terrestrial through the ministration of the celestial.
88 And also the telestial receive it of the administering of angels who are appointed to minister for them, or who are appointed to be ministering spirits for them; for they shall be heirs of salvation.
89 And thus we saw, in the heavenly vision, the glory of the telestial, which surpasses all understanding;
90 And no man knows it except him to whom God has revealed it.
91 And thus we saw the glory of the terrestrial which excels in all things the glory of the telestial, even in glory, and in power, and in might, and in dominion.
92 And thus we saw the glory of the celestial, which excels in all things—where God, even the Father, reigns upon his

throne forever and ever;
93 Before whose throne all things bow in humble reverence, and give him glory forever and ever.
94 They who dwell in his presence are the church of the Firstborn; and they see as they are seen, and know as they are known, having received of his fullness and of his grace;
95 And he makes them equal in power, and in might, and in dominion.
96 And the glory of the celestial is one, even as the glory of the sun is one.
97 And the glory of the terrestrial is one, even as the glory of the moon is one.
98 And the glory of the telestial is one, even as the glory of the stars is one; for as one star differs from another star in glory, even so differs one from another in glory in the telestial world;
99 For these are they who are of Paul, and of Apollos, and of Cephas.
100 These are they who say they are some of one and some of another—some of Christ and some of John, and some of Moses, and some of Elias, and some of Esaias, and some of Isaiah, and some of Enoch;
101 But received not the gospel, neither the testimony of Jesus, neither the prophets, neither the everlasting covenant.
102 Last of all, these all are they who will not be gathered with the saints, to be caught up unto the church of the Firstborn, and received into the cloud.
103 These are they who are liars, and sorcerers, and adulterers, and whoremongers, and whosoever loves and makes a lie.
104 These are they who suffer the wrath of God on earth.
105 These are they who suffer the vengeance of eternal fire.
106 These are they who are cast down to hell and suffer the wrath of Almighty God, until the fullness of times, when Christ shall have subdued all enemies under his feet, and shall have perfected his work;
107 When he shall deliver up the kingdom, and present it unto the Father, spotless, saying: I have overcome and have trodden the wine-press alone, even the wine-press of

the fierceness of the wrath of Almighty God.
108 Then shall he be crowned with the crown of his glory, to sit on the throne of his power to reign forever and ever.
109 But behold, and lo, we saw the glory and the inhabitants of the telestial world, that they were as innumerable as the stars in the firmament of heaven, or as the sand upon the seashore;
110 And heard the voice of the Lord saying: These all shall bow the knee, and every tongue shall confess to him who sits upon the throne forever and ever;
111 For they shall be judged according to their works, and every man shall receive according to his own works, his own dominion, in the mansions which are prepared;
112 And they shall be servants of the Most High; but where God and Christ dwell they cannot come, worlds without end.
113 This is the end of the vision which we saw, which we were commanded to write while we were yet in the Spirit.

The LDS church teaches that through the grace of God exalted humans, husbands and wives sealed to one another forever, will participate in the divine nature and exercise divine powers, including the power of creation—through remaining subordinate always to God.

Jesus clearly stated that there will be no marriage in Heaven (Matthew 22:30; Mark 12:25; Luke 20:35), but LDS doctrine disagrees and teaches that couples married in one of their temples are seal together for all eternity, even if the man has multiple wives.

Joseph Smith claims that the Lord revealed to him that the "same sociality which exists among us here will exist among us there [in eternity], only it will be coupled with eternal glory" (Doctrine and Covenants 130:2).

Hell

LDS believe that there is a hell, but it will be lightly populated. After all, once someone gets a taste of hell, only a fool would reject a second chance.

These sons of perdition (perhaps only few in number) will be resurrected but will not be redeemed from the power of Satan because they are still filthy; as the prophet Alma said of them: "… they shall be as though there had been no redemption made; for they cannot be redeemed according to God's justice; and they cannot die, seeing there is no more corruption." (Alma 12:18.)

All mankind will thus receive general salvation, excepting the sons of perdition. Following their resurrection, "they shall return again to their own place, to enjoy that which they are willing to receive, because they were not willing to enjoy that which they might have received." (D&C 88:32.)

Chapter 5

Jehovah Witnesses

Jehovah Witness started by "Pastor" Charles Taze Russell, who by the age of 16 had turned from the Presbyterian and Congregational churches to skeptic. He refused to accept the doctrine of Hell and founded what is now known as the Jehovah Witnesses. The movement started from a Bible study in Allegheny, Pennsylvania in the 1870's. Russell was elected "pastor" of the Bible study, even though he had never received any formal Bible training.

After leaving his job as assistant editor of a small monthly magazine, he founded his own periodical called *Zion's Watch Tower and Herald of Christ's Presence*. The magazine focused on the teaching that Christ was already present and had been since 1874. It was 1884 that Russell founded Zion's Watch Tower Tract Society and installed himself as president.

Russell followed in the teachings of William Miller, who taught that the return ("advent") of Christ would occur in 1843. When this did not happen, he changed the date to 1844. When Christ failed to return in 1844, some followers, like Russell, believed that Christ had done something crucial in 1844 but had done it invisibly in heaven. Russell taught that Christ's "presence' would climax in 1914 with God's judgment on all human nations (the end of the "Gentile times") and the establishment of the kingdom of God.

After the death of Russell, "Judge" Joseph F. Rutherford took over the helm in 1917, after a three-month power struggle. Rutherford adopted the name "Jehovah's Witnesses" for the organization. In 1939 the Society changed the name of its flagship publication from Zion's Watchtower and Herald of Christ's Presence to The Watchtower Announcing Jehovah's Kingdom.

These name changes reflected several developments. Most significantly, it reflected the Society's abandonment of most of Russell's chronology. The Society was forced to recon with the fact that WW I had failed to be Armageddon. They had no choice but to quietly abandon Russell's teaching that Christ's "presence" had become a reality in 1914. Instead, the Society began teaching that Christ's presence was a period of time beginning, rather than ending, in 1914. The society made this change only after every effort to extend the chronology beyond 1914 had failed (the most notable being Rutherford's claim that 1925 would mark the final date for worldly powers and the resurrection from the dead of Abraham, Isaac, Jacob, and others).

Authority

The Bible and the New World Translation

The Jehovah Witness's (JW's) believe that the Bible is divinely inspired and accurately transmits God's thoughts and will to mankind.

> There are many strand of evidence proving that the Bible really is God's Word. Each strand is strong, but when all are taken together, they are unbreakable. (*The Bible—God's Word or Man's*, 1989, p.12)

> Yes, the Bible is true, as so many, many examples prove. The Bible does not contain only true history. *Everything* it says is true. Even when it touches on matters of science, it is marvelously accurate. (emphasis original) (*You Can Live Forever in Paradise on Earth*, 1982, p.55)

The New World Translation of the Holy Scriptures (NWT) is the best translation of the Bible because it was accurately translated by faithful men.

> The endeavor of the New World Bible Translation Committee has been to avoid this snare of religious traditionalism. (*New World Translation of the Christian Greek Scriptures*, 1950, p. 6)

> Outstanding among Bibles is the *New World Translation of the Christian Greek Scriptures.* ... Accuracy, uniformity, clarity, and up-to-date language mark this excellent work. Bible study aids without equal make this an indispensable help to sincere searching students of God's Word. (*What Has Religion Done for Mankind*, 1951, p. 351)

The Watchtower Bible and Tract Society

There is only one true religious organization (administrated by the Watchtower Bible and Tract Society). Believers must submit to this one true organization even if it contradicts their long-held view or appears to them to be unbiblical.

> We acknowledge as the visible organization of Jehovah on earth the Watchtower Bible and Tract Society, and recognize the society as the channel or instrument through which Jehovah and Jesus Christ give instruction and meat in due season to the household of faith. (*Watchtower*, April 15, 1939, p. 125)

JW's believe that only the Watch Tower and Tract Society can correctly interpret the Bible because it is an organizational book that cannot be properly understood by individuals without the help of the organization through which God works (that is, the Watch Tower Society).

> The Bible is an organizational book and belongs to the Christian congregation as an organization, not to individuals, regardless of how sincerely they may believe that they can interpret the Bible ... the Bible cannot be properly understood without Jehovah's visible organization in mind. (*Watchtower*, October 1, 1967, p. 587)

> God has not arranged for that Word to speak independently or to shine forth life-giving truths by itself. ... It is through his organization God provides this light. (*Watchtower*, May 1, 1957, p. 274)

"Such a claim, which substitutes the organization for the Bible, means that no Christians in any age had access to scriptural truth until the Watch Tower Society began its work. Moreover, this claim relegates the direct help of the Holy Spirit in illuminating the text to either a minor or nonexistent role. This directly contradicts John 16:13 and 1 John 2:27. Moreover, Ephesians 1:17-18 states that the Spirit will provide wisdom and illumination to the revelation of God in the Bible. First Corinthians 2:12 says, *'We have not received the spirit of the world but the Spirit who is from God, that we may understand what God has freely given us.'*

"Paul indicates that one stands approved of God through diligent study of the Scriptures (2 Timothy 2:15). If Paul the apostle needed to be judged by the Scriptures by the Bereans (Acts 17:11), surely the teaching of the Watch Tower should be judged by the Word of God."[8]

> "Make haste to identify the visible theocratic organization of God that represents his king, Jesus Christ. It is essential for life. Doing so, be complete in accepting its every aspect." (*Watchtower*, October 1, 1967, p. 591)

> "To receive everlasting life in the earthly paradise we must identify that organization and serve God as part of it." (*Watchtower*, February 15, 1983, p. 12)

> "If we are to walk in the light of truth we must recognize not only Jehovah God as our father but his organization as our 'mother'." (*Watchtower*, May 1957, p. 274)

> "They [witnesses] must adhere absolutely to the decisions and scriptural understanding of the Society because God has given it this authority over his people." (*Watchtower*, May 1, 1972, p. 272)

> "Avoid independent thinking … questioning the counsel that is provided by God's visible organization … .Fight against independent thinking." (*Watchtower*, January 15, 1983, p. 22, 27)

> "So Jehovah's visible organization under Christ is a channel for bringing the diving interpretation of his word to his devoted people." (Watchtower, June 1, 1938, p. 169)

> "Unless we are in touch with this channel of communication that God is using, we will not progress along the road to life, no matter how much Bible reading we do." (Watchtower, December 12, 1981, p. 27)

> "Let us face the fact that no matter how much Bible reading we have done, we would never have learned the truth on our own." (Watchtower, December 1, 1990, p.19)

Publications

The New World Translation of the Holy Scripture

This is the bible published by the Watchtower Bible and Tract Society for the JW's. It was first published between 1950-1960, it was revised in 1961, and again in 1970. It was written to "restore" the name Jehovah in the Old Testament where the consonants "YHWH" appear. They also inserted the name in the New Testament where the text refers to the Father. The Watchtower society claims that it is the best translation available today.

The Kingdom Interlinear Translation of the Greek Scriptures

This was first published in 1969 and revised in 1985. It presents a reliable text of the Greek New Testament (the Westcott and Hort Greek text) and the Watchtower's word-for-word English renderings underneath on the left side of the page, with the NWT on the right.

Insight on the Scriptures

This is the JW's official Bible encyclopedia. It contains two volumes published in 1988.

Reasoning From the Scriptures

This is a topical handbook which answers the most commonly challenged Watchtower interpretations and teachings from the scriptures. It was published in 1985, revised in 1989. It is arranged alphabetically by topic. This is one of the JW's most important booklets.

Should You Believe in the Trinity?

This is a booklet that seeks to refute the doctrine of the Trinity.

Awake!

This is a semi-monthly magazine that targets mostly "unbelievers" and focuses on non-biblical trends and topics in society. There are nearly 13 million copies printed biweekly into 75 languages. It is designed to inform witnesses about current issues and attract non-Witnesses to the religion.

The Watchtower Announcing Jehovah's Kingdom

This is a semi-monthly magazine and chief means of instructing JW's in doctrine and practice. There are over 16 million copies printed into 120 languages biweekly.

Other Materials

There are numerous other small books and pamphlets used to introduce the teachings of the Watchtower society to prospective members and for conducting "Bible" studies with interested parties and newly baptized members.

God

The Triunity

JW's do not believe in a Triune God. They define Triunity as, "the doctrine, in brief, is that there are three gods in one: 'God the Father, God the son, and God the Holy Ghost,' all three equal in power, substance, and eternity" (*Let God Be True,* 1946 ed., p. 100). JW's believe that this is a demon created doctrine based on the fact that the word does not appear in the Scriptures.

> Nowhere in the Scriptures is even any mention made of a trinity. (*Let God Be True*, 1946 [1952 rev.], p. 111)

> The obvious conclusion is, therefore, that Satan is the originator of the Trinity doctrine. (*Let God Be True*, 1946 ed., p. 101)

The word Trinity does not appear in the Bible and neither does omnipresence, omniscience, Jehovah and many other words we use to help us understand and describe God. There are many theological words that are used both by Christians and JW's to express doctrines but the words are not explicitly found in the Scriptures. Just because human beings cannot understand the doctrine of the Triunity does not make it false. If God is greater then us we would expect that there are a great many things that we cannot understand about Him.

Notice that that JW's misdefine that definition of the Triunity as three gods in one god (*Let God Be True,* 1946 ed., p. 100). This makes an easy straw-man argument to refute as they do later on page 102. However, they themselves are not consistent, for in *Can Live Forever in Paradise on Earth*, 1982, page 39 they properly define the Triunity as "three persons in one God".

> "There can be no compromise with God's truths. Hence, to worship God on his terms means to reject the Trinity doctrine. It contradicts what the prophets, Jesus, the apostles, and the early Christians believed and taught. It contradicts what God says about himself in his own inspired Word." (*Should You Believe in the Trinity?*, 1989, p. 31)

> "Who is this wonderful God? Some persons say his name is Jesus. Others say he is a Trinity, although the word "trinity" does not appear in the Bible. According to the teaching of the Trinity, there are three persons in one God, that is there is 'one God, Father, Son and Holy Spirit'." (*You Can Live Forever in Paradise on Earth*, 1982, p. 39)

> "Sincere persons who want to know the true God and serve Him find it a bit difficult to love and worship a complicated, freakish-looking, three-headed God." (*Let God Be True*, 1946 ed., p. 102)

> "The Trinity doctrine was not conceived by Jesus or the early Christians." (*Let God Be True*, 1946 ed., p. 111)

> "Never was there a more deceptive doctrine advanced than that of the trinity." (*Reconciliation*, 1928, p. 101)

> "The plain truth is that this is another of Satan's attempts to keep God-fearing persons from learning the truth of Jehovah and his Son, Christ Jesus. No, there is no Trinity." (*Let God Be True*, 1946 ed., p. 111)

The Holy Spirit

JW's believe that the Holy Spirit is God's active force that accomplishes God's will and not a personal being. The Holy Spirit is described as an impersonal energy that God uses and that He gives to His people to empower them to obey Him. They believe only a force could fill many people at the same time.

> The holy spirit is the invisible active force of Almighty God that moves his servants to do his will. (*Let God Be True*, 1946 ed., p. 108)

The Bible does in fact describe the Holy Spirit as a person often in the Scriptures (John 14:16-17; 15:26; 16:13-14). The attributes of the Holy Spirit are one of a personal being (Romans 15:30; Ephesians 4:30). The JW's do not understand the Holy Spirit and how He could be omnipresent therefore they create a Holy Spirit they can understand.

> "A comparison of Bible texts that refer to the holy spirit shows that it is spoken of as 'filling' people; they can be 'baptized' with it; and they can be 'anointed' with it. (Luke 1:41; Matt. 3:11; Acts 10:38) None of these expressions would be appropriate if the holy spirit were a person." (*Reasoning from the Scriptures*, 1985, p. 380)

> "As for the 'Holy Spirit', the so-called 'third person of the Trinity', we have already seen that it is not a person, but God's active force." (*The Truth That Leads to Eternal Life*, 1968, p. 24)

> “The Scriptures themselves unite to show that God’s holy spirit is not a person but is God’s active force by which he accomplishes his purpose and executes his will.” (*Aid to Bible Understanding*, 1969, 1971, p. 1543)

> “The Bible’s use of ‘holy spirit’ indicated that it is a controlled force that Jehovah God uses to accomplish a variety of his purposes. To a certain extent, it can be likened to electricity, a force that can be adapted to perform a great variety of operations.” (*Should You Believe in the Trinity?*, 1989, p. 20)

> “No, the holy spirit is not a person and it is not part of a Trinity. The holy spirit is God’s active force that he uses to accomplish his will. It is not equal to God but is always at his disposition and subordinate to him.” (*Should You Believe in the Trinity?*, 1989, p. 23)

Jesus Christ

Pre-existence of Jesus Christ

Jesus Christ, before becoming man, preexisted in heaven as the first and only direct creation of God, known as Michael the Archangel. Before becoming man Jesus Christ was a mere angel. It was through this created archangel that God brought all other things into being. Michael, as Jehovah God’s greatest creation, was created first, and then he was used by God to create the rest of the universe

> 16For by him were all *other* things created, that are in heaven, and that are in earth, visible and invisible, whether they be thrones, or dominions, or principalities, or powers: all *other* things were created by him, and for him: 17and he is before all other things, and by him all other things consist. (Colossians 1:16-17 NWT)

> So the evidence indicates that the Son of God was known as Michael before he came to earth and is known also by that name since his return to heaven where he resides as

> the glorified sprit Son of God. (*Reasoning from the Scriptures*, 1985, p.218)

Although the JW's quote Colossians 1:16-17, it is important to note that they have added the word "other" to the text. The word "other" does not appear in the Greek text and the addition of the word dramatically changes the doctrine of the passage. In the first NWT they did not acknowledge that the word was added. However, in later revisions they had to place the word "other" in brackets to indicate that it was added to the Greek text for the English rendering. Even with this JW's claim that the NWT is the "best" translation.

While on earth Jesus was a perfect man, because it was God who transferred the life-force of Jesus to the womb of Mary.

> "Jesus, no more and no less than a perfect human, became a ransom that compensated exactly for what Adam lost—the right to perfect human life on earth. ... The perfect human life of Jesus was the 'corresponding ransom' required by divine justice—no more, no less." (*Should You Believe in the Trinity?*, 1989, p. 15)

Deity of Jesus Christ

Jesus Christ is not Jehovah God but instead "a god". This is seen in John 1:1 which states, "In the beginning the Word was, and the Word was with God, and the Word was *a god*" (emphasis added) (John 1:1 NWT). He was seen to be on earth as a perfect man and only spoken of as a god in that sense, as a perfect man, but no more and no less.

> The true Scriptures speak of God's son, the Word, as 'a god'. He is a 'mighty god', but not the Almighty God, who is Jehovah. (*The Truth Shall Make You Free*, 1943, 47)

JW's misunderstand the phase "Son of God" as an offspring of God. However, if you watch the reaction of the Jews when that phrase is used of Jesus Christ they want to stone Him for calling Himself God. The Jews, who lived at the time, understood that Jesus was calling Himself God, even if those today do not understand that terminology.

When Jesus is referred to as the "firstborn" it does not mean the "first created" but rather the superior one. In Jeremiah 31:9, Ephraim is called God's "firstborn son". However, Ephraim was not the first born child, Manasseh was the older. In this case we see that Ephraim was the firstborn in superiority over his older brother Manasseh.

> "In other words, he was the first and direct creation of Jehovah God." (*The Kingdom Is at Hand*, 1944, pgs. 46-49)

> "The Bible shows that there is only one God...greater than His Son...and that the Son, as the Firstborn, Only-begotten, and 'the creation by God', had a beginning. That the Father is greater and older than the Son is reasonable, easy to understand, and is what the Bible teaches." (*From Paradise Lost to Paradise regained*, 1958, p. 164)

> "Thus, Jesus had an existence in heaven before coming to the earth. But was it as one of the persons in an almighty, external triune Godhead? No, for the Bible plainly states that in his pre-human existence, Jesus was a created spirit being, just as the angels were spirit beings created by God. Neither the angles nor Jesus had existed before their creation." (*Should You Believe in the Trinity?*, 1989)

Resurrection of Jesus Christ

JW's believe that Jesus Christ was raised a spirit creature. They teach that Christ's human body was not raised from the dead. His body was dissolved into gasses or otherwise annihilated. Christ permanently forfeited his human life when he gave it up for a ransom. For Christ to have taken back human life would have meant that he was taking back the ransom price.

> Jehovah God raised him from the dead, not as a human Son, but as a mighty immortal spirit Son...For forty days after that he materialized, as angels before him had done, to show himself alive to his disciples. (*Let God Be True*, 1946 ed., p. 40)

The risen Jesus is obviously more than a man. Jesus has divine qualities and status. Jesus has divine qualities exactly representing God's (Colossians 2:9; Hebrews 1:3), and therefore must be a spirit (John 4:24). Jesus has supernatural abilities. Christ's invisibility proves him to be a spirit.

Jesus appeared in different bodies. The disciples often did not recognize him except by his actions.

> "This firstborn from the dead was raised from the grave, not a human creature, but a spirit." (*Let God Be True*, 1946 ed., p. 276)

> "Jesus did not take his human body to heaven to be forever a man in heaven. Had he done so, that would have left him a little lower than the angels…God did not purpose for Jesus to be humiliated thus forever by being a fleshly man forever. No, but after he had sacrificed his perfect manhood, God raised him to deathless life as a glorious spirit creature." (*Let God Be True*, 1946 ed., p. 41)

> "Usually they could not at first tell it was Jesus, for he appeared in different bodies. He appeared and disappeared just as angels had done, because he was resurrected as a spirit creature. Only because Thomas would not believe did Jesus appear in a body like that in which he had died." (*From Paradise Lost to Paradise Regained*, p. 144)

> "Having given up his flesh for the life of the world, Christ could never take it again and become man once more. For that basic reason his return could never be in the human body that he sacrificed once for all time." (*You Can live Forever in Paradise on Earth*, 1982, p. 143)

After the resurrection Jesus return to His original identity as Michael the archangel.

> "Read carefully the following Bible account: 'War broke out in heaven: Michael [who is the resurrected Jesus Christ] and his angels battled with the dragon.'" (*You Can Live Forever in Paradise on Earth*, 1982, p. 21)

JW's believe that Christ's invisible presence began in 1914. They believe that Biblical chronology in Daniel 4 points to the year 1914 as the end of the "Gentile times" or "appointed times of the nations" (Luke 21:24, NWT). Christ's prophetic discourse sets forth a composite "sign" of the end that has been evident since 1914. Wars, earthquakes, famines, pestilences, and lawlessness, among other ills, were to increase on a worldwide scale (Matthew 24:3-7, 12; Mark 13:7-8; Luke 21:10-11). The "good news of the kingdom," that is, the message that God's kingdom has come to power, was to be proclaimed in every nation (Matthew 24:14). This message has now been preached by Jehovah's Witnesses in nearly every nation on earth.

They state that Christ began ruling as king over the whole earth in 1914. From A.D. 33 until 1914 Christ had a kingdom, but its only subjects were the 144,000 (Colossians 1:13; Hebrews 12:22-24; 1 Peter 2:9-10). When Christ ascended to heaven, he had to wait a period of time before he could begin ruling over the earth (Hebrews 10:13; Psalms 110:1-6).

Sin

JW's believe that Adam's sin in the garden caused death and the condemnation is past on to all of his offspring. They would hold to a view of the original sin that is imputed to all people. JW's teach that all men have a sin nature.

> By the disobedience of Adam sin became active and he was sentenced to death, and condemnation resulted to all his offspring. Hence all were born sinners. (*Life*, 1929, p.194)

It is important to note in discussing the JW's view on the eternal state that they do not believe that man has an immoral soul. They believe that man is a soul not has a soul.

> Gen. 2:7: "Jehovah God proceeded to form the man out of dust from the ground and to blow into his nostrils the breath of life, and the man came to be a living soul. (Notice that this does not say that man *was given* a soul but that

> he *became* a soul, a living person.) (emphasis original) (*Reasoning from the Scriptures*, 1985, p.375)

Not only do JW's believe that man does not have a soul but is one, they also state that the doctrine of man having an immoral soul is from paganism.

> "'Man came to be a living soul'; hence man *was* a soul, he did not *have* a soul as something immaterial, invisible, and intangible residing inside him." (*Insight on the Scriptures*, vol. 2, 1988, pp. 1005-6)

> "How, then, did this belief about an immortal soul find its way into the teachings of Christendom's churches? Today it is about through the influence of pagan Grecian philosophy." (*Is This Life All There Is?*, 1974, p. 43)

Salvation

JW's believe that Jesus Christ's death on the cross was to pay the penalty of Adam's sin not the sins of all people. Once Adam's original sin was taken care of it makes the opportunity for all people to be rewarded with eternal life for their faith and good works. Faith is necessary in the sense that persons cannot or will not change their lives to obey God without faith. The basis on which God grants salvation is not simply believing or trusting God but "exercising faith" (John 3:16-18, NWT), that is, doing good works motivated by faith.

> To redeem or ransom man from the grave means that God will provide a means of satisfaction of the judgment against Adam." (*Life*, 1929, p. 206)

> Immortality is a reward for faithfulness. It does not come automatically to a human at birth. (*Let God Be True*, 1946 ed., p. 74)

Good works do not earn salvation, but they are prerequisites for it. The required works fall into four categories (*Watchtower*, February 15, 1983, p. 12-13).

1. "Taking Knowledge" of God and Christ (John 17:3, NWT) by studying the Bible (through the guidance of the Watchtower).

2. Obeying God's laws (meaning, all the rules laid down by the Watchtower).

3. Associating with God's channel, the Watchtower organization.

4. Participating in the Jehovah's Witness preaching work.

JW's believe that by Jesus Christ making payment for Adam's sin their good works can now count toward rewards. However, as we will see, if you are not saved you will not know it because the death of man is non-existence.

> "He [God] could not set aside the judgment that he had entered against Adam. He could, however, be consistent ... by permitting another to pay the debt of Adam and his offspring to be released from sin and death." (*Life*, 1929, p. 199)

> "It is for the reward of eternal life that every last person on earth should now be working. Are you?" (*Watchtower*, August 15, 1972, p. 492)

> "To get one's name written in that book of life will depend upon one's works, whether they are in fulfillment of God's will and approved by his Judge and King." (*Watchtower*, July 1, 1947, p. 204)

> "Those people of good will today who avail themselves of the provision and who steadfastly abide in this confidence will find Christ Jesus to be their 'everlasting Father' (Isaiah 9:6)." (*Let God Be True*, 1946 ed., p. 121)

> "We have learned that a person could fall away and be judged unfavorably either now or at Armageddon or during the thousand years of Christ's reign or at the end of the final test...into everlasting destruction." (*From Paradise Lost to Paradise Regained*, 1982, p. 241)

"Make haste to identify the visible theocratic organization of God that represents his king, Jesus Christ. It is essential for life. Doing so, be complete in accepting its every aspect." (*Watchtower*, October 1, 1967, p. 591)

"Jesus Christ identified a first requirement when he said in prayer. ... This means everlasting life, their *taking in* knowledge of you. ... Many have found the second requirement more difficult. It is to *obey God's* laws. ... A third requirement is that we *be associated with God's* channel, his organization. ... To receive everlasting life in the earthly Paradise we must identify that organization and serve God as part of it. The fourth requirement ... requires that prospective subjects of his Kingdom support his government by *loyally advocating his Kingdom rule to others* [that is, preaching door-to-door]." (*Watchtower*, February 15, 1983, p. 12-13)

Eternal State

JW's believe that there are three classes of people; the "little flock" which after death will reside in Heaven, the "great crowd" that will reside on Earth and the rest that will be non-existent.

Heaven

JW's believe that only 144,000, called the "little flock", will populate Heaven. These 144,000 are what the JW's say are the truly born-again children of God. They will be God's spiritual sons. They will be gods like Jesus Christ is a god.

"The Bible shows that only a limited number of persons, a 'little flock', will go to heaven." (*Watchtower*, February 15, 1984, p. 9)

"At the celebration of the memorial of Christ's death, only those who make up 'the Israel of God' should partake of the emblems of bread and wine." (*Watchtower*, March 15, 1983, p.9)

> "We are begotten of a divine nature. ... Jehovah is thus our father. ... We are divine beings—hence all such are Gods. ... Now we appear like men, and all die naturally as men, but in the resurrection we will rise in our true character as Gods." (*Watchtower*, December 1881, p. 3 [1919 reprint, p. 301])

Notice that the reward for the few (144,000) is they will be gods like Jesus Christ and the great crowd will serve them as gods. What was it that Satan said to Eve in the Garden (Genesis 3:5)? *"For God knows that in the day you eat of it your eyes will be opened, and* ***you will be like God****, knowing good and evil" (emphasis added).* The JW's hope to be part of the little flock that will be gods, just as Satan promised Eve. Also note that the JW's make a big deal about Jesus a little "g" god, yet in the quote above they claim they will be in their true character, which is God with a big 'G'.

> "The titles, Mighty God, and Everlasting Father ... are very appropriate to Our Lord Jesus. ... The same titles are applicable to the Church as his body." (*Watchtower*, November 1881, p. 10 [1919 reprint, pp. 297-298])

Earth

Those that make up the "great crowd" will live in the "Paradise earth" and serve the 144,000 in Heaven that make up the "little flock".

> "These dedicated, baptized 'other sheep' of the 'great crowd' have not been begotten to be God's spiritual sons, with a heavenly inheritance." (*Holy Spirit*, 1976, p. 157)

> "The rest of faithful humankind will live on earth as the subjects of these rulers." (*Watchtower*, February 15, 1984, p. 9)

> "The vast international company of 'other sheep' who do not partake, will enjoy everlasting life on the Paradise earth." (*Watchtower*, March 15, 1983, p.9)

Non-existence

JW's believe that when a person dies they completely cease to exist. There is no consciousness at all after death. Therefore, there cannot be a conscious eternal punishment for the "unbelievers". They believe that the "wicked" will be consumed in judgment and annihilated. They teach that hell is something that Satan made up.

> "The real roots of this God-dishonoring doctrine go much deeper. The fiendish concepts associated with a hell of toment slander God and originate with the chief slander of God (the Devil)." (*Reasoning from the Scriptures*, 1985, p. 175)

To what purpose would Satan gain by creating a doctrine of hell, that would if nothing else, scare them into looking for salvation? Satan would not create a doctrine of hell if a place of torment did not exist. Hell is the most popular reason people have for seeking salvation. Satan would be more likely to deny that such a place exists, much like the JW's do.

Note that JW's do not provide much incentive to becoming a JW, if they are right and we do not believe them, we will be without a consciousness and not know anything at all. However, the best they can offer is to live on earth as the servants of those in Heaven, since the 144,000 was full back in 1914.

> "The dead are shown to be 'conscious of nothing at all' and the death state to be one of complete inactivity. (Ec 9:5, 10; Ps 146:4). ... In both Hebrew and the Greek Scriptures, death is likened to sleep, a fitting comparison not only because of the unconscious condition of the dead but also because of the hope of an awakening through the resurrection." (*Insight on the Scriptures*, vol. 1, 1988, p. 597)

> "When a person is dead he is completely out of existence. He is not conscious of anything." (*You Can Live Forever in Paradise on Earth*, 1982, p. 88)

Chapter 6

Christianity

Authority

The authority for Christianity is Scripture alone.

The Bible is God's special self-revelation, which is limited in space and time and is directed to various designated individuals (2 Peter 1:21). The accepted books and writings that make up the Bible are the 39 Old Testament and 27 New Testament without any of the additional writings commonly known as the Apocrypha. The Bible provides the only inerrant and absolutely authoritative propositional knowledge of God that exists.

The authority of Scripture is God's self-revelation of One who has the right and power to command compliance in thought and action upon His rational creatures (Acts 17:30, 31; Romans 15:28). The Scriptures are our ultimate basis of authority for determining what is and who are right and wrong. Therefore, the Bible supremely defines what we are to believe and how we are to conduct ourselves. The Bible alone is authoritative for faith and practice.

Inspiration

The Bible is inspired by God. Inspiration identifies that supernatural work of the Holy Spirit in which He superintended (controlled and directed) the reception (to the writers) and communication (to the hearers and the writing) of the divine message to mankind such that the product (the original writing) is verbally (every word) and plenary (completely) both inerrant (without error) and authoritative (2 Timothy 3:16). God spoke in His written Word by a process of dual authorship. The Holy Spirit so superintended the human authors that, through their individual personalities and different styles of writing, they composed and recorded God's Word to man (2 Peter 1:20-21) without error in the whole or in the part (Matthew 5:18; 2 Timothy 3:16). Thus, the Scriptures are completely and totally sufficient for life and godliness.

Sufficiency

The Word of God is completely and totally sufficient for the believer in each and every area of life (2 Timothy 3:16). There is absolutely no human reasoning that needs to be added to or replace the Scriptures to make the needs of the believer for life and living. God commands that no part, no matter how small, should every be added nor subtracted from the Bible (Deuteronomy 4:2; 12:32; Proverbs 30:6; Jeremiah 26:2; Revelation 22:18-19). It is totally complete and sufficient for every area of life for every generation. The Scriptures are sufficient for life and godliness. The Bible constitutes the only infallible rule of faith and practice (Matthew 5:18; 24:35; John 10:35; 16:12 13; 17:17; 1 Corinthians 2:13; 2 Timothy 3:15 17; Hebrews 4:12; 2 Peter 1:20 21).

The only means of interpreting the Bible is a normal, grammatical, historical interpretation of Scripture which affirms the belief that the opening chapters of Genesis present creation in six literal days (Genesis 1:31; Exodus 31:17) and seeing a distinction between Israel and the Church. The Bible constitutes the only infallible rule of faith and practice (Matthew 5:18; 24:35; John 10:35; 16:12-13; 17:17; 1 Corinthians 2:13; 2 Timothy 3:15-17; Hebrews 4:12; 2 Peter 1:20-21). Whereas there may be many applications of any given passage of Scripture, there is but one true interpretation according to God. The meaning of Scripture is to be found as one diligently applies the normal grammatical historical method of interpretation under the illuminating of the Holy Spirit (John 7:17; 16:12-15; 1 Corinthians 2:7-15; 1 John 2:20). It is the responsibility of believers to ascertain carefully the true intent and meaning of Scripture, recognizing that proper application is binding on all generations. Yet the truth of Scripture stands in judgment of men; never do men stand in judgment of it.

God

There is one living and true God (Deuteronomy 6:4; Isaiah 45:5-7; 1 Corinthians 8:4), an infinite, all knowing Spirit (John 4:24), perfect in all His attributes, one in essence, eternally existing in three Persons: Father, Son, and Holy Spirit (Matthew 28:19; 2 Corinthians 13:14), each equally deserving worship and obedience.

Description

God orders and disposes all things according to His own purpose and grace (Psalm 145:8-9; 1 Corinthians 8:6). He is the Creator of all things (Genesis 1:1-31; Ephesians 3:9). As the only absolute and omnipotent Ruler in the universe, He is sovereign in creation, providence, and redemption (Psalm 103:19; Romans 11:36). He has an all-inclusive plan that He designed for His own glory all things that come to pass (Ephesians 1:11). He continually upholds, directs, and governs all creatures and events (1 Chronicles 29:11). In His sovereignty He is neither author nor approver of sin (Habakkuk 1:13; John 8:38-47), nor does He abridge the accountability of moral, intelligent creatures (1 Peter 1:17). He has graciously chosen from eternity past those whom He would have as His own (Ephesians 1:4 6); He saves from sin all who come to Him through Jesus Christ; He adopts as his own all those who come to Him (John 1:12; Romans 8:15; Galatians 4:5; Hebrews 12:5-9).

Triunity

The Triunity refers to the doctrine of the three Persons in one God. Some falsely, define this doctrine as three Persons in one Person or three Gods in one God. Both are incorrect. These false definitions are used by false teachers to make it easy to improperly refute this doctrine (i.e. a straw man argument). Properly defined, the Triunity is three Individuals, separate and distinct Persons in one completely and totally unified Godhead (1 John 5:7).

There are many intimations in the Old Testament of the Triunity. The use of the name of God; Elohim is a plural noun (Genesis

1:1). God also used plural pronouns to refer to Himself (Genesis 1:26; 3:22; Isaiah 6:8). These intimations support the plurality of the Godhead. The unity of the Godhead is evident in the use of the word “one” or in Hebrew “echad” (Deuteronomy 6:4). The word “echad” refers to unity not singularity.

Each of the Persons of the Triunity are objects of worship (Exodus 20:3; Matthew 14:33; John 4:24; 10:33; Luke 24:51-52; Philippians 2:9-11). They each possess all the attributes of God . Each Person is recognized as God (John 1:1; 16:27; Acts 5:3-4; 2 Corinthians 13:4; 1 Peter 1:2). Yet the plurality of the Godhead is distinct from each other (Genesis 1:1-2; 19:24; Psalm 45:6-7; 110:1; Isaiah 63:7,10; Hosea 1:7; John 14:16-17, 28; Galatians 4:4).

The concept of the Triunity is incomprehensible to man. All the attributes of God are fully true of each of the Persons or Essences of the Godhead. The doctrine of the Triunity is further proven in the Deity of Christ and the Deity of the Holy Spirit .

Jesus Christ

Jesus Christ, the second Person of the Triunity, possesses all the divine excellences, and in these He is coequal, consubstantial, and coeternal with the Father (John 10:30; 14:9). God the Father created according to His own will, through His Son, Jesus Christ, by whom all things continue in existence and in operation (John 1:3; Colossians 1:15-17; Hebrews 1:2).

Jesus Christ represents humanity and Deity in indivisible oneness (Micah 5:2; John 5:23; 14:9-10; Colossians 2:9).

Incarnation

In the incarnation (God becoming man), Christ surrendered only the prerogatives of deity but nothing of the divine essence, either in degree or kind. In His incarnation, the eternally existing second Person of the Trinity accepted all the essential characteristics of humanity and so became the God–Man (Philippians 2:5-8; Colossians 2:9).

Jesus Christ is virgin born (Isaiah 7:14; Matthew 1:23,25; Luke 1:26-35); He is God incarnate (John 1:1,14); and the purpose of the incarnation was to reveal God, redeem men, and rule over God's kingdom (Psalm 2:7-9; Isaiah 9:6; John 1:29; Philippians 2:9-11; Hebrews 7:25-26; 1 Peter 1:18,19).

Saviour

Jesus Christ accomplished our redemption through the shedding of His blood and sacrificial death on the cross and His death was voluntary, vicarious, substitutionary, propitiatory, and redemptive (John 10:15; Romans 3:24-25; 5:8; 1 Peter 2:24).

On the basis of the efficacy of the death of Jesus Christ, the believing sinner is freed from the punishment, the penalty, the power, and one day the very presence of sin; and he is declared righteous, given eternal life, and adopted into the family of God (Romans 3:25; 5:8-9; 2 Corinthians 5:14-15; 1 Peter 2:24; 3:18).

Our justification is made sure by His literal, physical resurrection from the dead and that He is now ascended to the right hand of the Father, where He now mediates as our Advocate and High Priest (Matthew 28:6; Luke 24:38-39; Acts 2:30-31; Romans 4:25; 8:34; Hebrews 7:25; 9:24; 1 John 2:1).

Jesus Christ is fully God. The Deity of Christ is asserted explicitly throughout the New Testament by many who recognized Jesus as God (John 1:1, 14; 20:24-29). The names of Christ dictates his Deity as God (John 1:1; 20:24-29; 1 Timothy 1:1; 4:10; Titus 1:3-4; 2:10, 13; 3:4, 6), "Lord" (Like 6:46; 24:24; Mark 2:23-28; John 13:13; Acts 10:36; 26:15; Revelation 19:6), "Son of God" (Matthew 16:16, Mark 1:11; 5:7; 15:39; John 10:31-39), "First and Last" (Isaiah 44:6; 48:12-13; Revelation 1:11, 17; 2:8; 22:13) and "I am" (John 8:57-59). The anticipated Messiah was described as God in the Old Testament (Psalm 2:7; Isaiah 7:14; 9:6; 40:3; Jeremiah 23:5-6; Micah 5:2).

For Christ to be God He must possess the attributes of God : incomprehensibility (Ephesians 3:8, 19), sovereignty (Romans 14:10-12), omniscience (John 2:24-25; 16:30-32), omnipotence (John 5:19, 21; Colossians 1:17), omnipresence (Matthew 28:20; Hebrews 4:13), immutability (Hebrews 13:8), eternality (John 1:1;

8:58; Revelation 1:8) and holiness (Mark 1:24). A Deity must do the works of God : creation (John 1:3; 1 Corinthians 8:6; Ephesians 3:9; Colossians 1:16; Hebrews 1:2), forgiveness of sin (Matthew 9:2-6; Mark 2:7), object of worship (Matthew 14:33; Luke 24:51-52; Philippians 2:9-11), source of life (John 10:28; 11:17; 37-44) and judgement (John 5:22, 27; Acts 10:42; 2 Timothy 4:1). The importance of the resurrection of Jesus Christ is that it has provides vindication for the Deity of Christ. If Jesus was not God then He would still be in the grave.

In the incarnation, the second person of the Trinity laid aside His right to the full prerogatives of coexistence with God, assumed the place of a Son, and took on an existence appropriate to a servant while never divesting Himself of His divine attributes (Philippians 2:5-8).

In the resurrection of Jesus Christ from the grave, God confirmed the deity of His Son and gave proof that God has accepted the atoning work of Christ on the cross. Jesus' bodily resurrection is also the guarantee of a future resurrection life for all believers (John 5:26-29; 14:19; Romans 1:4; 4:25; 6:5-10; 1 Corinthians 15:20, 23).

Jesus Christ will return to receive the church, which is called His body, unto Himself at the rapture, and returning with His church in glory, will establish His millennial kingdom on earth (Acts 1:9-11; 1 Thessalonians 4:13-18; Revelation 20).

Jesus Christ is the One through whom God will judge all mankind (John 5:22-23):

1. Believers (1 Corinthians 3:10-15; 2 Corinthians 5:10)

2. Living inhabitants of the earth at His glorious return (Matthew 25:31-46)

3. Unbelieving dead at the Great White Throne (Revelation 20:11-15)

As the Mediator between God and man (1 Timothy 2:5), the Head of His body the church (Ephesians 1:22; 5:23; Colossians 1:18), and the coming universal King, who will reign on the throne of

David (Isaiah 9:6; Luke 1:31-33), He is the final Judge of all who fail to place their trust in Him as Lord and Savior (Matthew 25:14-46; Acts 17:30-31).

Sin

Creation of Man

Man was directly and immediately created by God on the sixth day of creation, with appearance of age, in His image and likeness. Man was created free of sin with a rational nature, intelligence, volition, self-determination, and moral responsibility to God (Genesis 2:7, 15 25; James 3:9). Life of all men begins at conception. The spirit of man does not exist prior to conception. Men are distinct from angels in that they are a race and angels are not. This means that men cannot become angels and angels cannot become men. Men are distinct from both angels and God and will be for all eternity (1 Corinthians 6:3; Hebrews 1:14; 2:6-8; 12:22-24). Men are similar to angels in having a personality, but limited more so in power and abilities.

God's intention in the creation of man was that man should glorify God, enjoy God's fellowship, live his life in the will of God, and by this accomplish God's purpose for man in the world (Isaiah 43:7; Colossians 1:16; Revelation 4:11).

Sin Nature

The sin nature is that reality that has been imputed directly from Adam to every individual since Adam (except Jesus Christ) (Romans 5:12-19). The nature that each person, with the exception of Christ, possesses the sinful nature passed on from Adam to each generation. By this nature, all men are guilty of sin. The sin nature is inherited and each person is guilty of sin at the point of conception.

Every person has a sin nature and is totally depraved, in that they lack the proper affection and love toward God and they do evil. Total depravity, more importantly, refers to the fact that the whole of man was corrupted by sin, including man’s will. Inherited sin addresses the nature of man, where imputed sin addresses the reality of that nature imputed to each person from Adam.

Adam and Eve became sinners because they sinned. Where every person afterward sins because they possess a sin nature. After the fall, Adam and Eve committed sin because they now had a sin nature.

In Adam's sin of disobedience to the revealed will and Word of God, man lost his innocence; incurred the penalty of spiritual and physical death; became subject to the wrath of God; and became inherently corrupt and utterly incapable of choosing or doing that which is acceptable to God apart from divine grace. With no recuperative powers to enable him to recover himself, man is hopelessly lost. Man's salvation is thereby wholly of God's grace through the redemptive work of our Lord Jesus Christ (Genesis 2:16 17; 3:1-19; John 3:36; Romans 3:23; 6:23; 1 Corinthians 2:14; Ephesians 2:1-3; 1 Timothy 2:13-14; 1 John 1:8).

Because all men are in Adam, a nature corrupted by Adam's sin has been transmitted to all men of all ages, Jesus Christ being the only exception. All men are thus sinners by nature, by choice, and by divine declaration (Psalm 14:1-3; Jeremiah 17:9; Romans 3:9-18, 23; 5:10-12).

The results of Adam's sin were a three-fold death. Physical death, which is the separation of the body from the spirit, is the particular penalty of imputed sin. The second is spiritual death, which is the separation of the spirit from God (while living on earth), and particular to inherited sin. The last is eternal death, which is the separation of the body and spirit from God, and is the particular and final penalty for depravity. Eternal death is a penalty for all unforgiven sin: inherited, imputed, impaired, committed or omitted.

There are some objections raised that can be easily answered. First, there is the objection that there is no sin prior to consciousness. However, most sin is of nature rather than deliberate. Also, the first act of an infant is a self-act of desiring milk and the result is crying. That cry for milk is an act of selfishness, which is all an infant knows. Thus, the very first act of an infant is sinfully selfish although the infant is not conscious of sin.

The second objection is that we cannot be responsible for what Adam did. However, we are responsible for what we do, and because of Adam we have a sin nature, and therefore we sin. It is our sin that we are responsible for, to God. This can be followed with the objection that we cannot repent of Adam's sin. However, it is because of sin and not sins (plural) that we need to repent. Can we be guilty of all Adam's sins? Adam made one choice that gave him and every person to follow him a sin nature. We are not guilty of Adam's sins but our own sin.

Although Adam's one sinful act brought about a sin nature in that all sin, one righteous act of Christ brought about the availability for any to have His righteousness imputed to them. Where the sin nature is once to all, righteousness is once to few.

Depravity of Man

The depravity of man refers to man being completely and totally corrupted by sin. This depravity includes the will of man (John 8:34). Depravity is any lack of holy affection to God or any bias toward evil. Due to imputation of sin every person is a sinner and is depraved (Romans 3:10-23; 5:12). The depravity of man is a total depravity, not partial. This does not mean that an unsaved individual has no disposition or tendency to do good (John 8:9; Romans 2:14). A depraved sinner is not without some pleasing or religious qualities (Matthew 23:23; Mark 10:21). A person as totally depraved is not prone to commit every form of sin (Matthew 23:23; Romans 2:14; 2 Timothy 3:13). No sinner is as intense in sin as he could be (Genesis 15:16; Matthew 11:24; 2 Timothy 3:13).

Depravity is properly that a sinner is destitute of true love for God (John 5:42), elevates some lower affection above God (2 Timothy 3:4), prefers self to God (2 Timothy 3:2), is at enmity with God (Romans 8:7), corrupted in every faculty (2 Corinthians 7:1, Ephesians 4:18; Titus 1:15; Hebrews 3:12), can do nothing God can fully approve of (Isaiah 64:6; Romans 3:9; 7:18) and has a pervading tendency toward greater depravity (Romans 7:18, 23). Total depravity is not total inability. A sinner is restricted, but still is sovereign over that which God has placed man over. A sinner is limited and unable to change their course of life, prefer God to self, neither live above sin nor capable of performing any act fully acceptable to God.

Origin of Sin

The origin of sin was committed, at a minimum, by Satan (Isaiah 14:12-17; Ezekiel 28:11-19). Scripture does not state when the demons fell, whether it was with Satan or sometime after. Man's sin was by an historical act that God used to test man (Genesis 3). Satan's sin was the original sin of creation, man's sin was the original sin of the human race (Romans 5:12). Satan's sin was internal where man's sin was influenced by the serpent (Genesis 3). Adam's sin was deliberate, where Eve was deceived (1 Timothy 2:14).

The fall of Satan reveals that both man and angels were created with the ability to choose from moral alternatives. A desire to sin arose in Satan. The first sin was rebellion against God's authority and pride in both man's and the angel's potential. Both man and angels are fully accountable for their own sin. They were not tempted by God nor did He create sin (James 1:13).

Extent of Sin

The extent of sin affects all of creation. When Eve sinned the affects were not realized until Adam's sin (Genesis 3:6-7). Upon Adam's sin, the creation began to experience the effects of sin. By the time after the flood the full effects of sin on creation were experienced. The extent of sin in angels is seen in that they are confirmed in holiness or sinfulness for all eternity. The extent of sin in man is revealed in the depravity of man.

Imputation of Sin

Imputation of sin is the inheriting of the sin nature directly from Adam (Romans 5:12-19). This one act caused a sin nature in every man, even before there was a written law to explain the penalties. The immediate result of that one act of sin was death, physical, spiritual and ultimately eternal. This death has been passed on to everyone from generation to generation, even to those not conscience. Finally, that by this one act of sin there was also one act of righteousness by Christ that remedies the act of

Adam. The contrast in Romans 5:12-19 parallels the sin of Adam and the salvation of Christ. It reveals the similarities and differences between the two events in history. The sin of Adam was a real event and test in history, not a mythical account.

The parallels between Adam and Christ are seen in the "oneness". The result of Adam's sin was both physical and spiritual death. The "oneness" is revealed in the one sinful act of Adam and the one righteous act of Christ. The sin nature extends to all people, except Christ. Sin was brought into the world by one sinful act not acts. Thus, Christ's death was one act for one act not one act for many acts. Therefore, Christ died by one act for sin, not sins.

Due to Adam's one sin, all men are rightly judged for imputed sin. It is deserved and to all. However, grace is not to all men and completely and totally unmerited by men. Because of this, not all men are in Christ, but all men are born in Adam. The result of being in Adam is condemnation where the imputation of righteousness by being in Christ is redemption. Those in Adam have a certain death both physical and spiritual. However, those in Christ do not have a spiritual death any longer and may even avoid the physical death in the rapture.

Now that we see the parallels and differences we can see that there is a similarity and even more so a superiority between Christ and Adam. There is a similarity in all being "in Adam" and those "in Christ"; the one act of Adam and one act of Christ; the union with Adam and those in union with Christ. However, the superiority is in the nature of the one act of Christ, which can impute His righteousness to those who are in Adam. Christ's one act is the remedy for the result of Adam's one act. The important note between the similarity in oneness between Adam and Christ is in a "natural oneness" versus a "spiritual oneness". All men are in Adam (naturally) and some men are in Christ (spiritually).

The superiority can be seen in the contrast between Adam and Christ. Adam disobeyed and Christ obeyed. Adam's act was imputed to all men; Christ's righteous act is imputed to few men. Adam's act has the involvement and participation of each person and Christ's act has the involvement and participation of only Christ and not any man.

There is a contrast in union as described above in that Adam's is a natural union and Christ's is a spiritual one. The union with Adam is immediate at conception and the union with Christ is conditional based upon faith and regeneration. All suffer through Adam because of his act and only Christ suffered by His act.

No one can escape the imputation of sin but few receive the imputation of righteousness. Therefore, all men deserve of the imputation of sin and its judgment but none are deserving of the grace of God. Thus, all sin is merited and grace is completely unmerited.

Salvation

Salvation is wholly of God alone by grace alone because of the redemption of Jesus Christ alone, the merit of His shed blood, and not based on human merit or works (John 1:12; Ephesians 1:7; 2:8-10; 1 Peter 1:18-19).

Regeneration

Regeneration is a supernatural work of the Holy Spirit by which a new nature and eternal life are given (John 3:3-7; Titus 3:5). It is instantaneous and is accomplished solely by the power of the Holy Spirit through the instrumentality of the Word of God (John 5:24), when the repentant sinner, as enabled by the Holy Spirit, responds in faith to the divine provision of salvation. Genuine regeneration is manifested by fruits worthy of repentance as demonstrated in righteous attitudes and conduct. Good works will be its proper evidence and fruit (1 Corinthians 6:19-20; Ephesians 2:10), and will be experienced to the extent that the believer submits to the control of the Holy Spirit in his life through faithful obedience to the Word of God (Ephesians 5:17-21; Philippians 2:12b; Colossians 3:16; 2 Peter 1:4-10). This obedience causes the believer to be increasingly conformed to the image of our Lord Jesus Christ (2 Corinthians 3:18). Such a conformity is climaxed in the believer's glorification at Christ's coming (Romans 8:17; 2 Peter 1:4; 1 John 3:2 3).

Election

Election is the act of God by which, before the foundation of the world, He chose in Christ those whom He graciously regenerates, saves, and sanctifies (Romans 8:28-30; Ephesians 1:4-11; 2 Thessalonians 2:13; 2 Timothy 2:10; 1 Peter 1:1-2).

Sovereign election does not contradict or negate the responsibility of man to repent and trust Christ as Savior and Lord (Ezekiel 18:23, 32; 33:11; John 3:18-19, 36; 5:40; Romans 9:22-23; 2 Thessalonians 2:10-12; Revelation 22:17). Nevertheless, since sovereign grace includes the means of receiving the gift of salvation as well as the gift itself, sovereign election will result in what God determines. All whom the Father calls to Himself will come in faith and all who come in faith the Father will receive (John 6:37-40, 44; Acts 13:48; James 4:8).

The unmerited favor that God grants to totally depraved sinners is not related to any initiative of their own part nor to God's anticipation of what they might do by their own will, but is solely of His sovereign grace and mercy (Ephesians 1:4-7; Titus 3:4-7; 1 Peter 1:2).

Election should not be looked upon as based merely on abstract sovereignty. God is truly sovereign but He exercises this sovereignty in harmony with His other attributes, especially His omniscience, justice, holiness, wisdom, grace and love (Romans 9:11-16). This sovereignty will always exalt the will of God in a manner totally consistent with His character as revealed in the life of our Lord Jesus Christ (Matthew 11:25-28; 2 Timothy 1:9).

Justification

Justification before God is an act of God (Romans 8:33) by which He legally declares righteous those who, through faith in Christ alone, repent of their sins (Luke 13:3; Acts 2:38; 3:19; 11:18; Romans 2:4; 2 Corinthians 7:10; Isaiah 55:6-7) and confess Him as sovereign Lord (Romans 10:9-10; 1 Corinthians 12:3; 2 Corinthians 4:5; Philippians 2:11). This righteousness is apart from any virtue or work of man (Romans 3:20; 4:6) and involves the imputation of our sins to Christ (Colossians 2:14; 1 Peter 2:24) and the imputation of Christ's righteousness to us (1 Corinthians

1:30; 2 Corinthians 5:21). By this means God is enabled to "be just and the justifier of the one who has faith in Jesus" (Romans 3:26).

Sanctification

Every believer is sanctified (set apart) unto God by justification and is therefore declared to be holy and is therefore identified as a saint. Sanctification is positional and instantaneous and should not be confused with progressive sanctification. Sanctification has to do with the believer's standing, not his present walk or condition (Acts 20:32; 1 Corinthians 1:2, 30; 6:11; 2 Thessalonians 2:13; Hebrews 2:11; 3:1; 10:10, 14; 13:12; 1 Peter 1:2).

There is also, by the work of the Holy Spirit, a progressive sanctification by which the state of the believer is brought closer to the standing the believer positionally enjoys through justification. Through obedience to the Word of God and the empowering of the Holy Spirit, the believer is able to live a life of increasing holiness in conformity to the will of God, becoming more and more like our Lord Jesus Christ (John 17:17, 19; Romans 6:1-22; 2 Corinthians 3:18; 1 Thessalonians 4:3-4; 5:23). In this respect, every saved person is involved in a daily conflict, the new creation in Christ doing battle against the flesh, but adequate provision is made for victory through the power of the indwelling Holy Spirit. This struggle nevertheless stays with the believer all through this earthly life and is never completely ended. All claims to the eradication of sin in this life are unscriptural. Eradication of sin is not possible, but the Holy Spirit does provide for victory over sin (Galatians 5:16-25; Ephesians 4:22-24; Philippians 3:12; Colossians 3:9-10; 1 Peter 1:14-16; 1 John 3:5-9).

Security

All the redeemed, once saved, are kept by God's power and are thus secure in Christ forever (John 5:24; 6:37-40; 10:27-30; Romans 5:9-10; 8:1, 31-39; 1 Corinthians 1:4-8; Ephesians 4:30; Hebrews 7:25; 13:5; 1 Peter 1:5; Jude 24). It is the privilege of believers to rejoice in the assurance of their salvation through the testimony of God's Word, which, however, clearly forbids the use of Christian liberty as an occasion for sinful living and carnality (Romans 6:15-22; 13:13-14; Galatians 5:13, 25-26; Titus 2:11-14).

Separation

Separation from sin is clearly called for throughout the Old and New Testaments, and the Scriptures clearly indicate that in the last days apostasy and worldliness shall increase (2 Corinthians 6:14-7:1; 2 Timothy 3:1-5).

Out of deep gratitude for the undeserved grace of God granted to us and because our glorious God is so worthy of our total consecration, all believers should live in such a manner as to demonstrate their adoring love to God and so as not to bring reproach upon our Lord and Savior. Separation from all religious apostasy and worldly and sinful practices is commanded of us by God (Romans 12:1-2, 1 Corinthians 5:9-13; 2 Corinthians 6:14-7:1; 1 John 2:15-17; 2 John 9-11).

Believers should be separated unto the Lord Jesus Christ (2 Thessalonians 1:11-12; Hebrews 12:1-2) and affirm that the Christian life is a life of obedient righteousness that reflects the teaching of the Beatitudes (Matthew 5:2-12) and a continual pursuit of holiness (Romans 12:1-2; 2 Corinthians 7:1; Hebrews 12:14; Titus 2:11-14; 1 John 3:1-10).

Eternal State

Death

Physical death involves no loss of our immaterial consciousness (Revelation 6:9-11), the soul of the redeemed passes immediately into the presence of Christ (Luke 23:43; Philippians 1:23; 2 Corinthians 5:8), there is a separation of soul and body (Philippians 1:21-24), and for the redeemed, such separation will continue until the rapture (1 Thessalonians 4:13-17), which initiates the first resurrection (Revelation 20:4-6), when our soul and body will be reunited to be glorified forever with our Lord (Philippians 3:21; 1 Corinthians 15:35-44, 50-54). Until that time, the souls of the redeemed in Christ remain in joyful fellowship with our Lord Jesus Christ (2 Corinthians 5:8).

There will be a bodily resurrection of all men, the saved to eternal life (John 6:39; Romans 8:10-11, 19-23; 2 Corinthians 4:14), and the unsaved to judgment and everlasting punishment (Daniel 12:2; John 5:29; Revelation 20:13-15).

The souls of the unsaved at death are kept under punishment until the second resurrection (Luke 16:19-26; Revelation 20:13-15), when the soul and the resurrection body will be united (John 5:28-29). They shall then appear at the Great White Throne Judgment (Revelation 20:11-15) and shall be cast into hell, the lake of fire (Matthew 25:41-46), cut off from the life of God forever (Daniel 12:2; Matthew 25:41-46; 2 Thessalonians 1:7-9).

Heaven

There is a literal place known as heaven, where persons, both men and angels, will consciously worship God in the real, everlasting presence of God.

Hell

There is a literal place known as hell or the lake of fire, were persons, both men and angels, will be consciously punished, both body and soul, for their sin in a real, everlasting, tormenting lake of fire.

Endnotes

[1] Partridge, Christopher, *Introduction to World Religions;* Fortress Press, Minneapolis, MN; 2005 (Page 10).

[2] Cohen, A, *Everyman's Talmud.* (New York: Schocken Books Inc.;1975), pages 134-135.

[3] Cohen, pages xvii-xviii.

[4] Cohen, pages v-vi.

[5] Cohen, page 5.

[6] These persons were supposed to be generally unconscientious in the discharge of their duties.

[7] Sookhdeo, Patrick, *A Christian's Pocket Guide to Islam.* (Wiltshire, England: Isaac Publishing; 2001), pages 9-14.

[8] House, H. Wayne, *Charts of Cults, Sects & Religious Movements;* Zondervan Publishing House, Grand Rapids, MI 2000; p. 151.